"I absolutely love this book. It brings the stories of some of the greatest biblical heroes to life in a way that is relevant, reassuring (they were far from perfect), and revolutionary (their passion changed the world). By the end you'll feel like you've been hanging out with some of the most incredible people who ever lived."

Pete Greig. Author, Church leader and founder of 24-7 Prayer.

"With *Lifelines* Mike and Andy use their passion to see disciples raised up, their biblical insights and their very own inimitable style, to bring fresh insight and understanding. They are able to make the Bible manageable, and its people real, and everything so accessible. This is a wonderful book written by Spirit-inspired followers of Jesus, whose love for Him and for His followers emanates from every page. We are absolutely delighted to recommend it."

John and Eleanor Mumford. Co-ordinators of the Vineyard International Executive.

"Mike and Andy write and live with honesty, integrity and a deep faith in the God who heals, frees, equips and consistently uses ordinary people with extraordinary power. Every insight in this book is backed by their own lives. It's a must read for anyone seeking to live out their faith!"

Danielle Strickland. Speaker, author and campaigner.

"Mike and Andy are a gift to more than one generation, but their way of connecting with young people in post-Christian cultures is beyond rare. In a time when so many churches are emptying out, to see them rally thousands of students and young people around Jesus is a kind of embodied hope. I'm thrilled that Mike and Andy are writing Lifelines. They are the very thing they call all of us to be."

John Mark Comer. Author and Pastor of Bridgetown Church Portland.

ANDY CROFT AND MIKE PILAVACHI

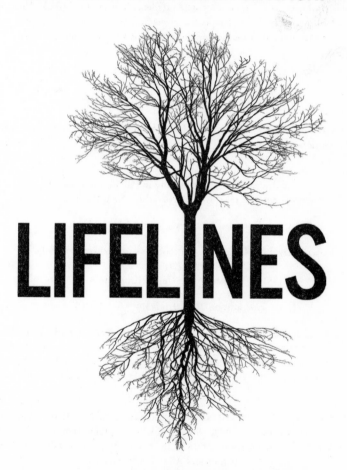

LIFELINES

SOUND ADVICE FROM THE HEROES OF THE FAITH

LIFELINES Published by David C Cook, 4050 Lee Vance Drive Colorado Springs, CO 80918, U.S.A.

Integrity Music Ltd., a division of David C Cook, Eastbourne, East Sussex BN23 6NT, United Kingdom

ISBN 978-1-4347-1186-1

British Library Cataloguing in Publication Data
A catalogue record for this book is available from the British Library

The Cook Team: Ian Matthews, Jennie Pollock, Abbie Robson

Cover Design: Mark Prentice, beatroot.media Cover image: Adobe stock
Typesetting by Zaccmedia
Printed in the United Kingdom

First Edition 2018 0 1 2 3 4 5 6 7 8 9 10

CONTENTS

DEDICATION

To Bishop David and Mary Pytches

Your example of encouragement, humility, faithfulness, boldness and love for Jesus mean more to both of us than words can ever say. Elisha had Elijah, David had both Jonathan and Samuel, Paul had Barnabas and Timothy had Paul. We have had you both praying for us, cheering us on, giving us your wisdom and the occasional gentle rebuke, and rejoicing with us in our victories whilst consoling us in our defeats.

We don't know who we would be without you in our lives. We love you.

ACKNOWLEDGEMENTS

We are very aware that this book, whilst it bears our names, was written in community. There are a number of friends who have their fingerprints all over these chapters, some of whom have paid a price as the two of us have locked ourselves away for sometimes hours on end to write these pages. We want to thank: all of our Church family at Soul Survivor Watford. You are kind, humble, compassionate, enthusiastic and faithful, and it is our privilege to serve you. We do not deserve you but we are so glad that we are going on this adventure together. Our dear friend Ali Martin who has, as always, given wise insights and corrections that have made this a better book than it would otherwise have been. Patrick Sinclair, you introduced Andy to Jesus and have been a faithful friend ever since. Thank you for reading the manuscript so willingly and giving both your encouragement and advice. Our thanks also to Jack Lewis who spent a number of flights reading through various chapters and spotting errors that we missed. We are grateful to Ian Matthews our publisher and Jennie Pollock our editor for their patience and kindness to us as we missed deadline after deadline, and for their dedication and wisdom.

Our thanks to our dear friends John and Debby Wright who kindly agreed to write the foreword. We love and admire you immensely.

Finally, and above all, we would both like to thank Beth, Josiah and Judah Croft. Beth, you are amazing. You have gone the fifth and sixth mile and more as Andy has been absent more than was ever intended. You are an amazing wife, mother and friend. Josiah and Judah, you have no idea how much joy you bring to your dad and your Uncle Mike.

FOREWORD

Mike and Andy have been dear friends of ours for many years, but that's not why we're writing this foreword! We are commending this book to you because it's a *really* great read, with deep, practical insights written in an extraordinarily accessible way.

What comes through so evidently is that these guys have not just studied the biblical characters within and mined valuable life lessons from their stories, but that they have 'walked the walk' themselves. Within these pages they share their own experiences with vulnerability, candour and self-deprecating humour, grounding the insights in instantly relatable twenty-first century reality.

It's an enjoyable read punctuated by the authors' amusing notes about each other, and even if you're not a big reader it's the sort of book you can dip into, as each chapter is complete in itself.

Whether you are new to faith or have been following Jesus for decades, we trust you'll find in these pages timeless truths which will deepen your walk with him.

John and Debby Wright
Pastors of Trent Vineyard, Nottingham
National Directors of Vineyard Churches UK & Ireland

INTRODUCTION

Therefore, since we are surrounded by such a great cloud of
witnesses, let us throw off everything that hinders and the sin
that so easily entangles. And let us run with perseverance the
race marked out for us...

Hebrews 12:1

Our host opened his front door with a warm smile that made his
eyes crinkle at the corners. He ushered us down the corridor of
his little bungalow into the study and busied himself making tea.
We settled ourselves into armchairs and after a moment were able
to take the measure of the man opposite us. He was small and
elderly. He had white hair, wire-framed glasses and a cardigan. He
looked friendly, affable and like one of the twinkly-granddad-types
used on adverts to sell dentures.

A glance around the study told another story. The shelves were
crammed with countless worn-out, carefully read books. The room
was strewn with fascinating looking objects clearly collected
throughout the world. And 'twinkly-granddad' had numerous

framed photos of himself with armed, well-known extremists. In the photos he was shaking hands with them as he gave them a Bible.

This was Brother Andrew.

We'd invited him to come and speak at one of our Soul Survivor events a few years before; he had agreed to come but cancelled at the last minute. We'd been upset until we discovered his reason: Brother Andrew had sneaked across the border into Afghanistan and was baptising a hundred new believers in a river. (He was in his seventies at the time.) This wasn't unusual for him. In fact, he'd spent a lifetime smuggling Bibles to the persecuted church and evangelising to drug barons, and now he felt God calling him to share the gospel with Islamic extremists. He wanted to go to the people no one else would try to reach.

We spent a happy two hours trying to get inside Brother Andrew's head. Here was a man who hadn't just 'lived it' (past tense); he was in his old age still *living it*. He was having wild adventures with God. He was 'all in' for Jesus. What were the most important lessons God had taught him over the years? How did he stay passionate? Did he ever doubt? Was he ever afraid? What were his biggest mistakes? Did he have any other dreams? *How could we become more like him?*

At the end of our time together Brother Andrew suggested we prayed. Mike clasped his hands together, screwed up his eyes and prayed one of his best prayers: 'God, thank you for all your gifts, help us to love everyone in the whole world, and bless the little children.' Andy felt Mike's prayer had covered all the bases, so backed him up with his most impressive-sounding '*Amen!*'

Then Brother Andrew prayed. Years later we still remember the words: '*God, I pray that you would help us to crawl on our bare hands and knees across a field of broken glass if, on the other side of that field, there is a single soul that might be saved for you.*'

The words were followed by a long silence. We knew that if we had prayed that prayer the words would have seemed empty. At that moment, however, as we sat in that study (with armed men watching us from within their photo frames), we knew Brother Andrew meant them. Of course Brother Andrew is not faultless, he is weak and sinful just like us, but his life is a demonstration of what it is to follow Christ. There are few things more inspiring and challenging than spending time with someone like him. In our experience, it doesn't just cause us to head out to foreign lands for crazy adventures; it inspires us to live the impossible right here at home. It helps us make sense of a life following God. It urges us onward, cheers us towards the finishing line and makes us want to run the best race we can for Jesus.

This book is about introducing us to a *crowd* of people like Brother Andrew. And what's more, we can spend time with them every day.

Lives That Speak Today

There are two reasons we have written *Lifelines*. The first is that we long to introduce a new generation of Christians to the Bible. It is our conviction that we have no hope of living a life of friendship with God and being changed into his likeness if we are not people who know our Bibles. Our first book, *Storylines*, used a wide-angle lens to look at the great themes of Scripture from Genesis to Revelation. In *Lifelines* we are putting different Biblical characters under the microscope. We would encourage you to read this book with the Bible in your other hand.

Secondly, whenever we open Scripture, the lives of those who have followed God before us 'surround us'. Though we are separated by millennia we wrestle with the same questions and face the same challenges. In this sense the Bible is full of people who can act as friends and guides. Of course we can't sit down with them as with Brother Andrew. Andy can't get John to give him fishing tips (biblical evidence suggests John couldn't have in any case). Mike can't ask Joseph to interpret his dreams (which, unlike Pharaoh's, seem to contain *only* fat cows). Yet in a way David *can* walk beside us. So can Ruth, Daniel, Mary and many others. Their lives can stir and shape ours; the race they ran for God can encourage us to run faster and truer.

We have found that the following witnesses have kept us company in the highs and lows of life and in the battles and blessings we've had as we follow Jesus. We pray and expect that they will do the same for you. Our hope is that in reading this book your life will be deeply impacted. You will know your identity secured, your worship enriched, your friendships improved and your heart encouraged.

CHAPTER 1

CHANGING YOUR SELF-IMAGE:
LESSONS FROM THE LIFE
OF JOHN

See what great love the Father has lavished on us, that we
should be called children of God! And that is what we are!

1 John 3:1

Jesus Changes People

It is often said that Jesus can change people. He can – dramatically.
There are many stories we could tell of his transforming power.
Here are just two:

Our first story is of a young man who struggled very badly with
self-image. He always felt different, as if he didn't really belong
anywhere. In his early teenage years he withdrew from meaningful
relationships and went through long periods where he couldn't even
have conversations with people. He would answer any questions
with a one-word 'yes' or 'no'. He got used to feeling lonely and
isolated from the world. Though things improved slightly in his
later teens, he would still withdraw from any relationship that

became at all difficult. He thought of himself as a 'big brown lump' and couldn't understand why anyone would want to be his friend.

One reason behind this was that his parents were immigrants to England. They hadn't taught him English so his first day at school had been a scarring experience. He was five years old, unable to speak the language and left in a playground of others who all seemed to be friends. His father would also often have violent mood swings and angry outbursts that would hurt him deeply. He grew up terrified of him.

This young man became a Christian and over time the love of Jesus began to heal him. He began to realise that God's love did not involve mood swings; that the love of his heavenly Father was dependable and consistent. He was amazed to discover that God actually wanted to spend time with him – he'd spent all his early years convincing himself that nobody really did.

Over the years God's love has restored him to the point where he can function in a far healthier way in relationships. As a result of receiving God's love he is able to be confident in other people's love for him. He would be the first to acknowledge that there is still a way to go but he would also say that he is astonished at the journey he has taken. He now wishes he could talk to his younger self and tell him not to worry, that it would all turn out okay.

The second young man grew up in a loving Christian family and yet somehow began to believe that love was conditional on him being successful, whether it be in education, sports or other ways. He learnt to work hard and his fear of failure drove him to attain a first class degree at Cambridge University – even though, by his own admission, he's not very bright. This fear meant that if he was put in a situation where failing was a distinct possibility he would become anxious. In his teens, he was intensely wounded by a relationship breakdown and remembers vowing to himself, 'I will never let anyone hurt me again.' As a result, from that time on he kept his distance emotionally from people and substituted genuine intimacy in friendships for a veneer of charm.

As he encountered Jesus he discovered that Jesus was vulnerable in his love and was willing to be hurt and wounded – ultimately on the cross. Over the years the love of God permeated his being. He began to soften, and discovered the joy of really being known and loved by others. He allowed his humanity to emerge from hiding. He recognised where his continuous fears came from and was able to face them as he grew in confidence in God's love for him. He would also say that he is still on a journey, but he is so grateful that Jesus' love has thawed him out. He can now give and receive love in a deep way with his wife, his children and his friends.

We know these stories are accurate – because they are ours. We have both found deep and lasting healing because of God's love. When we first met Jesus we were, in different ways, emotionally scarred and broken, but the love of Jesus has transformed us. This same transformation can happen for anyone who comes to know Jesus.

Our Great Need

If you were to hold a gun to Andy's head and a kebab to Mike's nose and say, 'What is the greatest need that you have seen in yourselves and in those around you?' we would say, without hesitation, 'The need to know that we are loved by God and to find our identity as children of the Father.'

Can you imagine what it would be like to know – deep in your heart – that you are accepted, delighted in, adored and have a purpose?

What difference would that make to you?

Picture waking each morning and being excited to live the day. Envision having an inner security about who you are. Visualise putting your head on the pillow and having a real, gut-level peace in your soul.

It's no overstatement to say that this truth revolutionises lives.

Am I Ugly?

As things stand many of us are struggling. Recent mental health statistics paint a bleak picture. Many are living life hamstrung by low self-esteem, self-doubt and fear. There are skyrocketing levels of anxiety, self-harm, depression and eating disorders. We are dealing with crippling levels of shame and guilt, constantly choosing to hide who we really are for fear of being 'found out'.

MIKE

A few years ago a friend suggested that I type into YouTube the words, 'Am I ugly? Tell me the truth.' He said I would be horrified and heartbroken. I was. I watched video after desperate video of young people – sometimes as young as ten – asking strangers, 'Am I ugly? Please tell me the truth; I have no one else to ask.' Some of the comments posted were, quite frankly, disgusting. Watching those videos made me realise how many of this generation struggle with issues of self-image and identity. It is a human tragedy in our midst.

Even when we aren't facing personal crises we often long to be different – to have more joy, greater meaning, to experience life in all its tantalising-but-seemingly-just-out-of-reach abundance. We battle to cope, or we puzzle over how to grasp the 'more' that always seems beyond us.

We the authors want to share what we have discovered: *The One who knows us the best loves us the most. We don't have to impress him; we can just rest in his love.* Jesus can truly be our centre, sustainer, lover, friend, redeemer, king and reason for living.

> The One who knows us the best loves us the most. We don't have to impress him; we can just rest in his love

Many of our destructive choices, low self-esteem and bad decisions come because we don't know this about Jesus. But if we *do* get it – *really get it in our guts* – healing, freedom and wholeness follow.

This is exactly what happened to a guy named John.

John's story is also one of radical change.

The Call of John

John and his brother James were fishermen at the Sea of Galilee. We're pretty sure John thought of himself as a failure. In those days the best of the best became rabbis. It was something every Jewish mother wanted for her son. Those who didn't make the cut had to find other employment – like catching fish.

Rabbis would select students to train up by heading to the Harvard of rabbinical schools. They would gather the students and ask themselves, 'Which of these has the potential to do what I do, and even greater things than me?' If they spotted someone promising they would point to them and say, 'follow me.' That person would then become their disciple. This reminds us of every teenager's nightmare: standing in a line and having two captains select (or not select) you to be on their football team.

Rabbi Jesus was different. He went to the Sea of Galilee, not the top rabbinical school. He pointed to John and his brother James and said, 'Follow me. Come and be part of my team.' This very act was probably the greatest affirmation that John had ever had. 'A rabbi chose me! He thinks I have potential!' Do you know that Rabbi Jesus has chosen you? He sees who you really are and what you can become.

Two Big-Shot Leaders

The two of us were recently invited to a meeting of 'strategic church leaders'. The agenda was to create prominent, powerful churches that could have significant influence. Needless to say we were rather pleased with ourselves for even getting an invitation. We dropped it into conversation with anyone who'd listen. (Our Uber driver didn't seem as impressed as he should have been.)

We continued feeling pretty smug until we saw a presentation about the sort of qualities that would be looked for in the leaders of these super churches. The presenter described the leader you might get if you crossed Mother Teresa and Steve Jobs with Nelson Mandela and Wonder Woman™. We slid lower and lower in our chairs as we measured ourselves against the endless list of attributes these potential leaders should have. By the time we left we knew we had been invited by mistake. Jesus has changed us and yet we're still a work in progress! If the people there really knew us they wouldn't have picked us. (Of course, we didn't tell them that.)

John – Really???

We can't help but wonder whether Jesus made a similar mistake with John. Did he know what he was doing when he invited him? What on earth did Jesus see in him?

James and John had a nickname: they were called 'Sons of Thunder'. This was not because they had digestive problems; it was almost certainly because they had bad tempers. On top of this, the gospels show us that John was selfishly ambitious, vengefully violent and excessively competitive.

John was selfishly ambitious, vengefully violent and excessively competitive

We might at the very least have expected Jesus to

back-track on John's selection once the flaws became obvious. In the modern workplace this is sometimes called 'beginning disciplinary proceedings'. In school it's referred to as 'behavioural measures'. Another way of putting it is, 'Three strikes and you're out!'

When we look closer at John's life it's not hard to find 'three strikes'.

Strike One: John was Selfishly Ambitious

A murder prediction

On several occasions while the disciples were travelling with Jesus he took them aside and talked about his coming death. In Mark 10:33-34, he warned them that when they arrived in Jerusalem he would be mocked, spat on, flogged and killed. Jesus didn't just say this 'by-the-by', he went into graphic detail; he made clear just how horrific it would be. Imagine a close friend telling you as you journey towards London that they know they will be brutally murdered there. You would at the very least be concerned and want to comfort and console them.

James and John, however, who evidently hadn't been on a counselling course (and seem to have had zero emotional intelligence) said to him, 'Teacher, we want you to do for us whatever we ask.' They went on, 'Let one of us sit at your right and the other at your left in your glory' (Mark 10:35, 37). The big request was not, 'Please, please don't die,' it was, 'Can we have the best seats in heaven?'

Unbelievable!

An equivalent might be you turning to your friend after the blow-by-blow description of their impending murder and saying, 'Would you mind leaving me the house in your will?'

So often we talk to Jesus in the same way John did: 'I want you to do whatever I want. And if you don't I'll be offended – it is a well-known fact that *I am the centre of the universe.*' Even worse, when Jesus said he was going to die a gruesome death, he meant he was going to die *for John.* He was going to pay the price for his sin and selfishness. So often we come to God upset because he hasn't given us what we want – that job, partner, or exam result – when, just like John, we haven't grasped the price he paid to give us everything that really counts.

Selective hearing

Jesus, surprisingly, did not respond to their request with the words, 'SHUT YOUR MOUTHS YOU MORONS I'VE JUST TOLD YOU I'M GOING TO DIE!' He said to them, 'What do you want me to do for you?' (Mark 10:36). How amazing! *Even when we ask the wrong things, with the wrong motives, he listens to us.* His goal is not to shame us, but to transform us. Although Jesus corrects and challenges us at the right time, the 'right time' is not always right away.

> *His goal is not to shame us, but to transform us*

One of our mentors is Bishop David Pytches. He has raised four amazing daughters.

Some years ago Mike asked David, 'What's your secret to bringing up children?' David leant over conspiratorially and whispered, 'Selective hearing.' He then explained that he took care to choose the right moment to confront his daughters about wrong attitudes or wrong behaviour. Any parent knows that love sometimes means keeping your mouth shut. If as a parent we are pointing out every fault, mistake and bad attitude, we won't see transformation, we'll see despair.

In asking for the best seats in heaven, James and John were seeking prominence. They wanted to be above everyone else, to be 'significant'. This attitude is as common today as it was then. We're searching for significance through things like growing a social media platform, getting that promotion or cultivating the perfect look. Though we're often not aware of it, our hunt for significance and position is usually a result of feeling insignificant. We don't know who we are, we don't understand who we were created to be, and we're trying to construct a meaningful identity for ourselves.

Our hunt for significance and position is usually a result of feeling insignificant

Jesus replied, 'You do not know what you are asking.' It's easy to miss this sentence; it's a profound response. How many of the prayers we offer up do we understand the consequences of? John's question came from a place of selfish ambition. He was so full of desire for his own glory, he had no space to appreciate that following Jesus is about laying down our lives; it's about surrendering them.

The way up is down

Jesus asked them a key question: 'Can you drink from the cup I'm going to drink from?' James and John said they wanted to be with Jesus in the place of glory. His response was, 'You do not understand the price that I'm going to pay *before* I can be in the place of glory. Do you really think you can get there on the cheap? If I am your rabbi, you've got to suffer and serve and be poured out, as I am.'

When the other ten disciples heard about John and James' request, they were angry with them. No doubt they suspected the two brothers were trying to elbow their way to the top. Selfish ambition always destroys relationships. There was a real danger of this happening here. Jesus intervened; typically, he didn't just give them a lecture about serving but said to them, 'I came not to be served but to serve, and to give my life as a ransom for many'. In other words, he said,

He said, 'My sermon is 'Serve One Another'; the illustration is my life. Look at me'

'My sermon is "Serve One Another"; the illustration is my life. Look at me.' With Jesus the way up is down.

Were we Jesus at this moment, we would definitely have regretted picking John for our team.

But it gets worse.

Strike Two: John Was Vengefully Violent

On another occasion Jesus sent messengers ahead of him to a Samaritan village. The Samaritan villagers refused to host Jesus – they wouldn't even offer him tea and digestives. The brothers' response is worth noting: 'When the disciples James and John saw this, they asked, "Lord, do you want us to call fire down from heaven to destroy them?"' (Luke 9:54). We might consider this a slightly over the top response! We don't burn down our neighbours' houses because they haven't invited us for lunch.

We then read, 'But Jesus turned and rebuked them' (v. 55). How we would love to know what he said to the brothers! We suspect it may have been something like this:

'Guys, I *knew* you were sleeping during the Sermon on the Mount! Burning a village because they wouldn't give us a cup of tea isn't exactly what I meant when I said "pray for those who persecute you!" Were you on your phones when I talked about turning the other cheek and loving your enemies?'

Why did John and James react in this way? Why does anybody react in a vengeful and violent way that is *out-of-proportion* to what has happened?

There's no more destructive human being than a hurt human being. Hurting people hurt people

First – we're hurting. There is a saying: 'the most dangerous tiger is a wounded tiger.' When a tiger is wounded is when it can cause the most destruction and damage. The same is true of people. There's no more destructive human being than a hurt human being. Hurting people hurt people.

Second, we have a fragile self-image. We are easily offended when our view of ourselves is delicate. Often, as in the case of the brothers, we like to think we are superior to others. Any perceived hurt or disrespect and our egos react like tender skin when it's been punched – we are instantly bruised. John wasn't big enough to let it go. He wanted to lash out, not because of what had been done to him, but because of his own insecurity.

Third, we're prejudiced. There were centuries of antagonism and hatred between Jews and Samaritans. A male Jew would pray every day for a good day, their daily bread, for safety and that there would be no Samaritans in the resurrection on the last day. We'd be surprised if intolerance that deep had skipped James and John. Plenty of people rejected Jesus – not least the Jewish elite – but this is the only group the brothers suggest burning alive! Prejudice always stems from our own brokenness. It's much easier to be tolerant, merciful and understanding of others when you are comfortable in who you are.

Strike Three: John was Excessively Competitive

On one level there's nothing wrong with being competitive. The two authors compete in sport (squash, tennis, weight lifting etc.), in wit and intellectual pursuits, and for the affections of Andy's children. This is, on the whole, good-natured competition and so Andy does not have a problem always losing.[1]

There is a competitiveness that is fun and brings people together. There is, however, a kind that is destructive and involves putting others down. This is often the result of an unhealthy comparison with others.

We catch a glimpse of this in John 20. Mary Magdalene has just informed the disciples that Jesus' tomb is empty. We read, 'So Peter and the other disciple [John] started for the tomb. Both were running, but the other disciple outran Peter and reached the tomb first' (vv. 20:3-4).

Stop and think about this comment. They are in the process of discovering that Jesus has risen from the dead, and John can't help but tell us that he is a faster runner than Peter! It would be as inappropriate and ludicrous as if Andy was to tell you in this book that he has won many more squash games than Mike over the years.[2]

To make matters worse, John actually closes his gospel by telling us that there are many of Jesus' miracles that he hasn't included. He says if he'd included them all, 'even the whole world would not have room for the books that would be written' (John 21:25). In other words, in order to stick to his word count,

---

1   Mike wrote this sentence.

2   He has.

John *omitted* many miracles of Jesus – but he still *chose to include* the fact that he is a faster runner than Peter! Sometimes competitiveness that comes out of insecure comparison causes us to make poor judgements.

John Was Transformed!

Put yourself in Jesus' position. You have picked someone to be part of your elite team:

1. You confided in them about your impending death. They immediately asked for the best seat in heaven. *Strike One.*
2. You explicitly preached about loving your enemies. They suggested setting them on fire. *Strike Two.*
3. You gave them the task of writing Scripture. A story of their athletic prowess is now in the Bible. *Strike Three.*

– Out!

Except, of course, that isn't what happened.

The reason it didn't happen is this: Jesus didn't choose John in order to use him. He chose him because he loved him. That is so important we'll repeat it: Jesus chose John because he loved him. This is where Christianity begins and ends: a relationship of love.

> *Jesus didn't choose John in order to use him. He chose him because he loved him*

Our Father does not see us as a means to an end, he doesn't grade us, he doesn't distribute his blessing according to our gifts or abilities. He simply loves us.

Transforming Love

'God's love changes us' sounds so like a cliché it can be tempting to dismiss it as 'A nice idea but not one that will ever really impact my life'. Love, however, has a profound and tangible effect on us.

Joel Holm, a friend of ours, tells a wonderful story. Some years ago he and his wife adopted a seven-year-old boy, Michael. Michael came from a desperate background – in his entire life he had never lived with any family for more than a few months. He had been passed from foster home to foster home and had been rejected repeatedly.

For the first months after he arrived little Michael was as good as gold. He did everything he was asked. He tidied his room. He was always polite. Joel's friends complimented him on his adopted son's behaviour. Nevertheless Joel knew that something was seriously wrong. He would often stand outside Michael's room after he put him to bed and hear his new son crying into his pillow. It broke his heart.

One night Joel went into Michael's room when he was asleep. He sat next to Michael's bed and looked at him. Waves of compassion came over Joel as he looked with love on his sleeping boy. He was broken by the thought that a seven-year-old could have gone through so much pain. Joel began to weep. After a while he noticed that Michael had woken up and was staring wide-eyed at him. The look on his face said, 'Are you really crying over me?' Joel picked up his boy and hugged him and then laid him down to sleep.

A few days later mum and dad took Michael to McDonald's. Joel asked him what he wanted and Michael replied, 'A Big Mac and large fries.' Joel said 'I'll get you the Big Mac but just small fries because you're only seven – that's all you'll manage to eat.' When he brought the order to the table Michael looked at the small bag of fries and in a fit of rage smacked them all over the floor. Surprisingly, his mum and dad were delighted! They wanted to pick all the fries up, put them back in the bag and say to Michael, 'Do it again!' Why did they react like this?

Joel says at that point he knew Michael finally understood he was loved. For the first time in his life he didn't have to try and be perfect so that he wouldn't be sent away. He had the confidence to throw a tantrum knowing that his dad loved him and would not reject him.

When we open our eyes as Michael did, and realise that the same Jesus who wept over his friend Lazarus, and wept over Jerusalem, weeps over us, things begin to change. The point is not that discovering God's love means we should throw more tantrums, but that when we are secure in God's love we won't be

We might get a hundred strikes, but we'll always and only ever be 'in'

afraid to throw tantrums for fear of him withdrawing his love. We won't feel like we need to tiptoe around God and be on our best behaviour. We will know, on good days and bad days, he is committed to us. The assurance that this brings revolutionises our relationship with God and our relationships with others. We might get a hundred strikes, but we'll always and only ever be 'in'.

Becoming Real

Again, to say 'love changes us' might seem simplistic, especially as we use the word 'love' to describe how we feel about music we like, clothes we wear and food we eat. But when we are talking about the love of Jesus we mean 'love' in a very particular way.

One of the best ways we know to describe this love is through a story Mike has enjoyed since childhood – *The Velveteen Rabbit*, by Margery Williams. It was first published in 1922, so the language is a little dated. The story is of a stuffed rabbit made of velveteen given to a little boy as a Christmas present. One night the rabbit finds himself talking to the oldest and wisest toy in the nursery, the Skin Horse, who shares a secret with him:

> 'What is Real?' asked the Rabbit one day, when they were lying side by side near the nursery fender, before Nana came to tidy the room. 'Does it mean having things that buzz inside you and a stick out handle?'

> 'Real isn't how you are made,' said the Skin Horse. 'It's a thing that happens to you. When a child

loves you for a long, long time, not just to play with, but REALLY loves you, then you become Real.'

'Does it hurt?' asked the Rabbit.

'Sometimes,' said the Skin Horse, for he was always truthful. 'When you are Real you don't mind being hurt.'

'Does it happen all at once, like being wound up,' he asked, 'or bit by bit?'

'It doesn't happen all at once,' said the Skin Horse. 'You become. It takes a long time. That's why it doesn't happen often to people who break easily, or have sharp edges, or who have to be carefully kept. Generally, by the time you are Real, most of your hair has been loved off, and your eyes drop out and you get loose in the joints and very shabby. But these things don't matter at all, because once you are Real you can't be ugly, except to people who don't understand.'

'I suppose you are real?' said the Rabbit. And then he wished he had not said it, for he thought the Skin Horse might be sensitive. But the Skin Horse only smiled. 'The Boy's Uncle made me Real,' he

said. 'That was a great many years ago; but once
you are Real you can't become unreal again. It lasts
for always.'[3]

The great secret of the nursery is that love – a very specific type of
love – makes you real. The same is true of us. 'Real' isn't how we
are made, it's something that
we become. As humans, being
physically born is simply the
beginning of coming alive;
the rest, strange as it may
seem, depends on love. Our
birth begins a journey to
becoming (or not becoming)
who we have been made to be.

> 'Real' isn't how we are made, it's something that we become

Another way of saying we
become 'Real' might be to say we are 'made whole' or that we discover
deep peace or inner security. *No one* simply grows these traits; they
are developed in a very particular way. *We are loved into life.*

For this to really happen this love has to have depth; it cannot
be a skin-thin 'like' online. It isn't a love that plays around
the edges of who we pretend to be most of the time. It has to go
to the heart of who we really are – to know us, even at our worst,
and stay anyway. This love has to be steadfast over a long, long
period of time – generally by the time you are 'Real' most of your
hair has been loved off and you are loose in the joints and very
shabby (on this count Mike is nearly there).

---

3   Margery Williams, *The Velveteen Rabbit* (William Heinemann Ltd,
1983) 4-5.

This love is so transformative – it's impossible to label yourself 'ugly', 'fat', 'stupid', 'a failure' when you have discovered it. You quite literally *cannot be ugly* (except to people who don't understand).

Instead, you start to give yourself a new label.

That label is Loved One.

At first, John was labelled the 'Son of Thunder'. After spending three years with Jesus, John gave himself a *new* label, a new title; he called himself 'the beloved disciple' (John 13:23; 19:26; 20:2; 21:7; 21:20). The one who had the nickname 'bad tempered one' renamed himself the Loved One!

He went on to write some of the Bible's most famous passages on love:

> Dear friends, let us love one another, for love comes from God. Everyone who loves has been born of God and knows God. Whoever does not love does not know God, because God is love ... Dear friends, since God so loved us, we also ought to love one another ... God is love. Whoever lives in love lives in God, and God in them. (1 John 4:7-8, 11, 16)

What an astonishing turnaround! Statements like this are so far from wanting to roast people alive it is almost impossible to believe the same person says both.

Our experience has been that sometimes, even with years of counselling, it's hard for us to ditch old labels. Usually we can't just shake off our negative attitudes or our unforgiving approach towards others. Radical inner transformation isn't possible simply by gritting our teeth. But John experienced this level of inside-out change.

What was the key to John discovering a new, healthier and – crucially – more accurate identity? Nothing more and nothing less than receiving every day the unconditional love of Jesus.

The Beloved Disciple

When we first noticed that John calls himself 'the disciple whom Jesus loved' we thought, 'How boastful!' We've since realised John didn't say this as an arrogant statement, but as a statement of joyful truth. When we get to a similar place – a point where we are able to call ourselves '[Insert your name here], whom Jesus loves' – everything will change.

 ANDY

When I started dating my wife, Beth, I was on my best behaviour. I paid for everything. I cracked my joke (there's only one). I wore my best clothes and even bought some expensive aftershave. After some time, I couldn't keep it up. Once, early in our relationship, we had a big argument. I had turned up in a terrible mood to meet some of her friends. They were kind and enthusiastic. I was non-reciprocal, talking in monosyllabic grunts between checking my phone for messages. Beth was not impressed. She made that clear to me, instructing me to never do it again. Then, to my great surprise, she carried on dating me! The months passed and every time I let her down, or she discovered another of my many flaws, or I forgot to wear the aftershave, I expected her to drop me. Eventually the penny began to drop: 'Oh my word. She's not going anywhere. She really loves me. This is for real.'

How Did Jesus Love John?

Jesus listened to John. He laughed with him and hung out with him. When John made his most stupid comments or behaved in a disgraceful way, Jesus didn't reject him, he forgave him. He served John, washed his feet and cooked him breakfast. He did miracles with and through John. He shared his life with him – it's no accident that it's John's Gospel that records Jesus' words, 'I no longer call you servants, because a servant does not know his master's business. Instead, I have called you friends, for everything that I learned from my Father I have made known to you' (John 15:15). We imagine John marvelling at hearing those words for the first time – 'He calls me "friend!"'

At the last supper John leaned against Jesus' chest. This was a sign of closeness and intimacy. In this moment he may literally have felt the heart of God's Son beating for him. In Jesus' death – when his heart ceased to beat – John witnessed first-hand the inestimable extent of his friend's love for him. After all, it was Jesus who had told him, 'Greater love has no one than this: to lay down one's life for one's friends' (John 15:13). It was perhaps this revelation of love that led him to write the best-known verse of the Bible; 'For God so loved the world that he gave his one and only Son, that whoever believes in him shall not perish but have eternal life' (John 3:16).

Jesus never said to John, 'Okay, here's your one year review, you've not come up to scratch, you're fired! Humphrey is going to take your place.' He loved him to the end and beyond. When John gave himself the label 'Loved One' it wasn't wishful thinking on his part. Somewhere along the road with Jesus he really began to believe it was true. One day he must have thought, 'Oh my word, I've been a total idiot *and he's still here*. He's giving no indication that he's going to walk away from me. I must really be the one he loves!'

Receive This Love

There came a moment when little Michael realised his new dad loved him. There was a point at which Andy knew Beth loved him in a deep way. The biblical word for this type of realisation is 'revelation.'

Receiving revelation is not like trying hard to understand a difficult maths equation. It's more like something inescapably dawning on us, like the sun rising. It happens *to us* and we couldn't 'unsee' it even if we wanted to. It's when God makes his truth clear to our hearts. Paul prayed for this for the Ephesians – 'I pray that the eyes of your heart may be enlightened in order that you may know the hope to which he has called you' (Eph. 1:18).

This type of revelation doesn't usually happen in an instant; it often takes time. The penny drops, but it's as if it drops in slow motion. When someone 'loves you for a long, long time, not just to play with, but REALLY loves you, then you become Real.' For John it didn't happen in minutes, days or months; it took years.

Mike loves food of every kind. In the spring he gets very excited and runs into his garden when the first tiny apples appear on the apple tree. He has been known to pick and eat a very little apple in May (not a good experience). He has realised that fruit takes a season to grow, mature and ripen. It's exactly the same with us.

Andy regularly visits the gym. There are days where he says to himself, 'I've been working really hard lifting weights and I can't notice my biceps getting bigger.' The joy Andy feels when he meets someone who hasn't seen him for six months and that person says, 'Wow, what has happened to your arms?' is hard to describe. Andy then goes back to the mirror, flexes, compares, and realises that the hours have paid off. (For the sake of integrity: Mike hasn't noticed this occurrence in his own life yet.)

We can sometimes become discouraged, and say to ourselves, 'I've prayed regularly and read my Bible for the last week, and I haven't noticed any difference; I still doubt

Spend time in his presence for three years, and then look in the mirror. You will see a different reflection

God's love for me!' All we can say, with all our hearts – and we are sure that John agrees with us – is spend time in his presence for three years, and then look in the mirror. You will see a different reflection.

Becoming a Christian by saying yes to Jesus begins a lifelong journey. There will be high points along the way: the Last Supper and the Cross must have been 'Aha!' moments for John. Lights can be flicked on in an instant. But the 'sun rising' and much of John's gradual realisation would have come in the ordinary hum-drum of life with Jesus. If we spend every day with Jesus as John did, if we worship him, listen and talk with him, go on adventures of faith with him, then the reality of Jesus' love will begin to permeate us. The accumulation of a thousand 'little moments' will move us. We will begin to realise that even after our worst mistakes Jesus doesn't fire us. He will never reject us, forsake us or stop loving us. Knowing this, we will wake each day a little different.

The Old Green Coat

In 1955 a lady called Elizabeth Henson was clearing out her wardrobe. She found an old green coat. It was ragged, frayed and faded. She decided its time had passed and went to throw the coat in the bin. To her surprise her son stopped her and asked if he could have the coat instead. She must have wondered why anyone would want something so tattered, but her son insisted. In the quiet of his room he worked on the rag. He cut it up and sewed it back together. He took a table tennis ball, cut it in half, and added it to the green coat.

Over the years Elizabeth Henson's discarded coat became a global pop icon, a movie star and dated the most glamorous pig on the planet. Out of that rag, Jim Henson created Kermit the Frog ™.[4]

Jim saw something that no one else could – the beauty behind the brokenness.

If Jim Henson can create a banjo-playing frog out of a discarded green coat, God can create something beautiful out of our imperfect lives. He won't just patch us up, mending a few holes; he'll take us far further. That's exactly what happened in this lifeline. Wandering by the Sea of Galilee, Jesus found John, a bad tempered, selfish, bigoted fisherman. And Jesus' love changed him; it made him whole, it made him Real.

The way this transformation happens is not by our striving to be better; it is by seeing ourselves through the eyes of our Father

This is exactly what Jesus will do for each of us. He sees who we were originally created to be before sin, hurt and despair marred us. He has a vision for our lives – that we become wholly who he has made us to be. The way this transformation happens is not by our striving to be better; it is by seeing

---

4   We are indebted to Mike Foster's brilliant book, *The People of the Second Chance* (Waterbrook, 2016), for this illustration.

ourselves through the eyes of our Father. It is by realising we have a new name. To him, we are the Loved Ones.

Read John's Lifeline for Yourself

John's story is woven throughout the gospel accounts. Here are a few key events:

- The call of John, Matthew 4:21-22
- The 'best seats' in heaven, Mark 10:35-45
- At the Samaritan village, Luke 9:51-55
- At the Last Supper, John 13:21-27
- At the cross, John 19:25-27
- At the tomb, John 20:1-10

You can also read about John's adventures in Acts, particularly chapters 3 and 4. He also wrote a lot – the books attributed to him are John's Gospel, 1, 2 and 3 John, and Revelation.

Group questions

1. Can you name an experience in life that has shaped the way you see yourself, either negatively or positively?
2. What are the main obstacles that prevent us from receiving the knowledge of God's love for us?
3. Can you recount a time when you had a revelation of the love of God for you?
4. How has the knowledge of God's love changed you?
5. What destructive labels do we put on ourselves?
6. What labels do you think our Father wants us to wear? Name five words that the Bible tells us God is speaking over us.

_____

CHAPTER 2

WHEN GOD SEEMS DISTANT: LESSONS FROM THE LIFE OF ELIJAH

And after the fire came a gentle whisper. When Elijah heard it, he pulled his cloak over his face and went out and stood at the mouth of the cave.

1 Kings 19: 12-13

Conference Jet-Lag

Have you ever returned from a Christian conference where you've had an amazing time? The friend you invited became a Christian. The teaching was so phenomenal you actually took notes. You had a powerful sense of God's presence as you worshipped him. Everything was incredible for those few days; yet just a short time after getting home you are utterly depressed. You have a row with someone in your family. You aren't even sure if *you* exist, let alone whether God does. We have both been there. Many times.

Most of us find relationship with God easy at an event, surrounded by thousands, but we struggle to sustain this in 'normal life'. More than once the two of us have thought, 'What's wrong with us? How is it that we can go from being so passionate to being so discouraged?' We've considered the options: perhaps we're hypocrites; maybe we're not up to the challenge; maybe we're the odd ones out and everybody else is on a permanent spiritual high. We've realised, however, that our reaction is probably quite normal.

If you are struggling to connect with God in the everyday then this chapter is about why that might be and what we can do about it. It's comforting to know that we are not alone – in fact, we are in highly exalted company.

Elijah was one of God's giants, a prophet *par excellence*. He lived around 860 BC and was God's man of faith and power. All the other prophets lived in his shadow; miracles would happen wherever he turned up. At Elijah's command there was a three-year drought (1 Kings 17:1). Ravens brought Elijah food to sustain him in the wilderness (1 Kings 17:6). (Having read about this Mike was once found in his garden begging the birds to feed him.) At Jesus' transfiguration it was Elijah who appeared with him. Elijah raised the dead, defied kings, defeated God's enemies and thunderously proclaimed God's truth to a people who had lost their way. Yet we suspect that the greatest lesson he learnt as he followed God was about encountering him not on the 'mountain tops' of life, but in the valleys.

Victory!

We join the story in 1 Kings 18. Israel had reached a low point. King Ahab had married a foreigner, Jezebel. This wouldn't be controversial today but in Israel it was against God's law. God knew they would be easily led into idol worship and this is exactly what happened. Queen Jezebel's idol of choice was called Baal. Over time she turned not only Ahab but the nation of Israel against the Lord.

Enter the man of God. The venue: Mount Carmel. In the red corner is Elijah the prophet. In the blue corner are the 450 prophets of Baal. The people of Israel are watching from the spectators' gallery.

'Then Elijah said to them, "I am the only one of the LORD's prophets left, but Baal has four hundred and fifty prophets"' (v. 22).

Elijah announced it was *one* against *four hundred and fifty*. The whole tone behind this declaration was, '*and I like the odds!*' He invited Baal's prophets to 'battle'. This 'battle' involved both teams preparing a bull to be sacrificed. They would then take turns to invite their gods to send fire from heaven on the bull. Whichever god answered with fire – he was the real God.

Baal's 450 prophets prepared their bull. They danced and cried out to Baal all morning. Nothing happened.

'At noon Elijah began to taunt them. "Shout louder!" he said. "Surely he is a god! Perhaps he is deep in thought, or busy, or traveling. Maybe he is sleeping and must be awakened"' (v. 27).

Thousands of years later can you hear the sarcasm? Can you hear the cocky confidence? This is the Muhammad Ali of Old Testament prophets! Baal's prophets became more frantic; they shouted louder, cut themselves with swords and did everything they could think of to attract Baal's attention. They kept at it all afternoon. The response? It is stated three different ways for us: 'But there was no response, no one answered, no one paid attention' (v. 29). It was a total failure. The people spectating, perhaps enthusiastic at first, must have stood in increasing silence until the exhausted prophets of Baal finally called it a day.

Then it was Elijah's turn. He repaired the altar of the Lord and prepared his bull. To make a statement, he then dug a trench and ordered the people to drench the bull in water, not once or twice but three times. The water saturated the sacrifice and filled the trench – not a good way to light a barbecue. Then Elijah stood back and delivered his knockout punch, a simple confident prayer: '"Answer me, LORD, answer me, so these people will know that you, LORD, are God, and that you are turning their hearts back again." Then the fire of the LORD fell and burned up the sacrifice, the wood, the stones and the soil, and also licked up the water in the trench. When all the people saw this, they fell prostrate and cried, "The LORD – he is God! The LORD – he is God!"' (vv. 37-39).

Fire fell; it even licked up the water – Elijah triumphed! The 450 prophets of Baal were put to death. As an encore Elijah called an end to the three-year drought.

Ladies and gentleman, it doesn't get better than this! It has to have felt better than preaching a great sermon would feel to Andy, or eating a great lasagne would feel to Mike. It was a victory that we can only dream about!

Songs of Victory to Thoughts of Suicide

Yet in the very next chapter we read this: 'Elijah was afraid and ran for his life. When he came to Beersheba in Judah, he left his servant there, while he himself went a day's journey into the wilderness. He came to a broom bush, sat down under it and prayed that he might die. "I have had enough, LORD," he said. "Take my life; I am no better than my ancestors"' (1 Kings 19:3-4).

Just let that sink in for a moment. *'Elijah was afraid and ran for his life.'*

He had just won an incredible victory. God had used him in a remarkable way. He had faced down massive odds. What was he afraid of? One angry queen. When she heard about her prophets Jezebel had sent Elijah a message: 'May the gods deal with me, be it ever so severely, if by this time tomorrow I do not make your life like that of one of them' (v. 2).

Bear in mind that Jezebel had just lost 450 prophets. The power of Baal had been utterly broken. It was surely an empty threat! Yet Elijah ran scared. We can't understand how Elijah went from the top of Mount Carmel to the bottom of a valley, sitting under a broom tree, praying that he might die. That is until we remember how we have felt the day we get home from Soul Survivor. We have seen many people become Christians, miraculous things have happened and we've encountered God in a powerful way, yet we often feel flat.

We Need Rest

Eat[5]

Elijah fell asleep. While he was sleeping God sent two angels from
the heavenly catering corps. When Elijah awoke there was fresh
bread baked over hot coals and a jar of water. 'Get up and eat,' an
angel told him (v. 5). Note that the angel didn't say, 'Get up and
pray more, fast more, give more, evangelise more, worship more.'
Elijah slept again, was woken and was given more food and drink.
This second time the angel said, 'Get up and eat, for the journey
is too much for you' (v. 7).

—————————————— MIKE ——————————————

When I was a young youth leader I went through a phase of being
exhausted emotionally, physically and (it felt) spiritually. I felt very
low. I went to see a wise mentor of mine called Barry, told him how
drained I was and asked, 'What should I do?' I fully expected him
to say, 'You need to pray more, read your Bible more, fast occasion-
ally and do the works of the kingdom.' Instead, he told me to go
home, get a Chinese takeaway, watch a movie and have some time
off. If I had paid for the advice I would have asked for my money
back! I thought, 'How unspiritual!' It turned out to be just what I
needed. Once I had rested physically my perspective changed;
I found it easier to pray, to enjoy reading my Bible and to spend

---

5   If you like this subheading there's an even better one coming up …

myself for others. God knows that we're human beings – we need rest, we need relaxation, we need Sabbath. He made us like that and I discovered He is as much present in our resting as in our praying.

A mistake we often make when struggling to connect with God is that we try to be more spiritual than he is

A mistake we often make when struggling to connect with God is that we try to be more spiritual than he is. The truth is it's very hard to pray when you are completely exhausted. If you find yourself in a place where God seems distant, worship is difficult and even being kind to the cat is challenging, *the problem may not be that you are a spiritual weakling who needs to try harder.* Another possibility is that you are running on empty. You may simply be physically or emotionally exhausted. Admitting this can be surprisingly hard.

———————————

Hitting 'the wall'

——————— ANDY ———————

Shortly before my thirtieth birthday, I hit a wall. I had been in ministry for eight years and running flat out the entire time. I loved it. I have always been aware I have one life; I want to spend it well.

I had heard stories about 'burnout' and people had warned me to be careful to take time off. I nodded my head, but in practise largely ignored them. Burnout was for other people; I was young, healthy and driven. As it turned out, I was also naïve. After years of neglecting healthy work-life patterns alongside shouldering more and more responsibility it finally came to a head. After an especially stressful few months I found myself sitting in a meeting when I suddenly felt my chest tightening. I struggled to breathe. I had an overwhelming urge to get up and run out of the room. I fought it and kept going till the end of the meeting. Then I called Mike – something was really not right.

To cut a long story short I began experiencing anxiety. It felt crippling and humiliating. I found the simplest tasks, such as replying to an email or making a phone call, overwhelming. In the space of a week I went from leading a church to watching daytime TV. I remember buying books on burnout and reading until three or four in the morning about others in church leadership who had found themselves in similar situations. Each had a common thread – people had underestimated the drain of ministry and of life. They had poured themselves out (with good intentions) until there was nothing left. Things then caught up with them: some had affairs, others allowed years of built up resentment and anger to get the better of them and still others began to experience panic attacks or depression. Many left full-time ministry.

One of the most helpful articles was by Bill Hybels. He leads a church of many thousands in Chicago, called Willow Creek. He spoke of a time when he found himself repeatedly crying for no obvious reason. He was desperate to quit church leadership. I could relate! Hybels had always monitored his wellbeing with two 'gauges' – his physical health and his spiritual health. During this time he realised there was a third gauge, the emotional gauge. He realised that whilst he was physically and spiritually fine he was emotionally totally depleted. Understanding this simple point helped me make sense of how I had ended up in such a state. We know that Elijah was physically exhausted. It wouldn't be surprising if he were also emotionally at the end of himself.

One of the most difficult aspects of emotional depletion is that we can't just snap out of it. Hybels describes our emotional levels as like a car battery – once flat recharge takes a long time. With most challenges, I had been used to gritting my teeth and pushing through. It was shocking, disconcerting and embarrassing not to be able to do so this time. I ended up having a month off work, receiving counselling and eventually starting back slowly. At the time of writing – a year later – I am on the road to recovery but still having to be disciplined about taking things slowly. If this experience has taught me anything it is to respect my human limitations.

There is only one Limitless One; we're made to depend on him rather than pretend to be him

There is only one Limitless One; we're made to depend on him rather than pretend to be him.

So you feel distant from God? You aren't praying much? Perhaps you are lacking in self-control or can't seem to read your Bible? Elijah teaches us it may just be that you've been running flat out for a long time. Too often we separate the physical and emotional from the spiritual – the 'secular' from the 'sacred.' God doesn't do this.

―――――――――――

Snacks Are Biblical[6]

Elijah's naps and snacks aren't an isolated incident in the Bible. Throughout Scripture people are *commanded* to live lives of regular rest. God himself rested after creating the world – a little like Andy when he finally assembles some IKEA furniture. The God who rests then orders his people to do likewise (Gen. 2:2; Ex. 20:8-11). To 'Sabbath' (*shabbat*) means 'to cease from doing' or even 'to celebrate'.

The pattern continued with Jesus. He turned water into wine and fed five thousand people at least in part because he cared about their physical bodies! He understood his own physical needs and filled his 'three years to save the world' with meals, parties and naps. 'Consider the lilies,' he said, 'look at the birds,' – the implication being he had slowed down enough to do so himself (Matt. 6:28, 26 NRSV).

―――――――――――

6   Mike's life message.

One of our favourite stories from the Gospels is when Jesus appeared on the shore of Lake Galilee after the resurrection. The disciples had been fishing all night and caught nothing. They were wet, hungry and tired. Jesus shouted out some pointers, a hundred and fifty-three fish were caught, the penny dropped and the disciples rushed to shore. Jesus was waiting for them with some fish already sizzling on the BBQ. How good that must have looked, smelt and felt to hungry, cold, wet fishermen! How unbelievably kind of Jesus – who had just been through the horror of the cross – to make cooking the disciples breakfast his first priority. Jesus went on to have a momentous conversation with Peter but we're clearly told it was 'when they had finished eating' (John 21:15). He made sure Peter was warmed up and had a full belly before they chatted.

'We don't become more spiritual by becoming less human'

Bread and sleep came first for a worn down Elijah, and breakfast for a weary Peter.

Elijah teaches us that, to quote Eugene Peterson, 'We don't become more spiritual by becoming less human.' Don't be more 'spiritual' than Elijah. Don't be more 'spiritual' than Jesus. If you are feeling very low, if God seems distant, eat some chocolate and get an early night (at least before you do anything else). It's not that God reluctantly 'allows' this; we think he encourages it.

We Need to Hear God

The Place of Encounter

Strengthened by this food and sleep Elijah travelled for forty days and nights to Mount Horeb. If Carmel is the mountain of 'victory', Horeb is the mountain of 'encounter'. This is the mountain of the burning bush, the place where the Lord met with Moses (Ex. 3:1-3). Elijah spent the night in a cave, and then 'the word of the LORD came to him: "What are you doing here, Elijah?"' (1 Kings 19:9).

We have to assume that the Lord knew exactly what Elijah was doing there! However, God sometimes asks questions to help *us* realise what is going on. Elijah's answer is revealing. It was not, 'Hey Lord, I've just had an amazing victory over the prophets of Baal! Did you see their faces when you sent the fire? Nice touch evaporating the water in the trench! You'll be pleased to hear that as a result the people have turned back to you. Oh, and then I got a bit scared of Jezebel so now I'm here.'

Instead Elijah says: 'I have been very zealous for the LORD God Almighty. The Israelites have rejected your covenant, torn down your altars, and put your prophets to death with the sword. I am the only one left, and now they are trying to kill me too' (v. 10).

Do you see what is missing? It's as if Mount Carmel never happened! As though Elijah's been convincing himself for the last forty days that it never took place. How easily we forget the things God has done in our lives! We can meet with God profoundly on one day and doubt him the next. We are so quick to return to old habits and thought patterns. Elijah repeats his statement from Mount Carmel, '*I am the only one left*', but while at Carmel it was said with triumph; here it is said in despair.

Interestingly the Lord doesn't start by giving Elijah a pep talk, but allows him to voice his fears. Then the Lord tells Elijah to go and stand on the mountain, 'for the LORD is about to pass by' (v. 11). A great wind passes by, then an earthquake and then a fire. We are told that the Lord was not in any of them. Then came a gentle whisper; when Elijah heard this he knew it was the Lord and left the cave.

Why the special effects? If God was planning to reveal himself in the whisper, why go to the effort of creating wind, an earth-quake and a fire first? God is teaching Elijah an absolutely crucial lesson – a lesson that if we don't learn we will never be able to live the Christian life. If we think we can survive on conferences, rallies or even Sunday services we are in for a great shock. These moments won't sustain us any more than the fire on Carmel sustained Elijah. Elijah was being taught that God's presence is not found simply in the earthquake, wind and fire moments of life.

God is present in the gentle whisper.

Why a Whisper?

We usually fail to hear God not because he isn't speaking, but because we're not listening. Or, more accurately, we're listening out for the wrong thing. Both of us would have headed out of the cave

Most of us are wired to hunt for the spiritual in the spectacular

the moment the earth began to shake or the wind began to blow – and definitely when we felt the heat of the flames. After all, hadn't God just arrived in fire on Carmel?

We imagine you might have done the same. This is because most of us are wired to hunt for the spiritual in the spectacular. We want to receive a stunning prophetic word, an overwhelming feeling of love, or a miraculous healing. We are not listening to *God* as much as we are looking for showy signs and dramatic revelations. We've boxed God into speaking impressively and missed that he prefers to speak lovingly. In doing so, we're too busy searching the sky for fireworks to notice God whispering in our ear. We need to learn to recognise the still small voice.

We've boxed God in to speaking impressively, and missed that he prefers to speak lovingly

God whispers because his priority is intimacy, not entertainment. You don't have to be close to the earthquake, wind or fire to feel its effects, but to hear the gentle whisper you have to feel his breath on your neck. It is this closeness that sustains us, that turns God's servants into his friends.

If the main thing you want is to be *used* by God then settle for spectacular moments a few times a year.

God whispers because his priority is intimacy, not entertainment

If, however, you want *deep relationship* with God, the gentle whisper is essential.

Be a Goldfish (Not a Camel)

Too many of us have treated encountering God like a camel treats finding water: filling up at a rare oasis and hoping to survive the long desert treks in between. Instead we're made to be goldfish, living *in* the life-giving water of God's presence. Whilst camels need to search for water, goldfish just need to recognise it's surrounding them. God *is* speaking to us. He wants to be near us. The key is to recognise this and then learn to tune our hearts to his.

There are two simple, practical things that we can do: withdraw to be alone with God, and 'practise the presence' of God in day-to-day life.

Getting Alone with God

— ANDY —

Some years ago I heard that spending time in silence was a good way to hear God. Apparently, in the second and third centuries a group who became known as the 'Desert Fathers' had retreated into the deserts of Egypt and received great revelations of God. It sounded promising ...

Deserts are hard to come by in Watford, so I booked myself into a local nunnery. I hired a hut in their garden for four days and headed there with just my Bible. My plan was to eat lunch daily with the nuns and fast the rest of the time. In this way I was sure I'd have some amazing revelations of my own.

I did.

After some time it was 'revealed' to me that sitting by yourself in a hut for days is mind-numbingly boring. As time went on it was also 'revealed' to me that when you are fasting between lunches you spend most of the time asking whether it's lunchtime yet. A particularly elderly nun told me she'd been in the nunnery for over sixty years; I found myself wanting to team up and plan a prison-break with her. At this point it was 'revealed' to me that my spiritual retreat was not going according to plan.

On day three I cracked. I called my wife; she came and collected me. That night, over what felt like the best curry I'd ever eaten, I decided that silent retreats were over-rated. I vowed, 'Never again!' But I have since done it again, and I loved it. With hindsight I've learned that a four-day cold-turkey retreat may have been trying to run before I could walk. If you want to run a marathon you start with getting off the sofa.

More recently I was asked a question that stuck with me: 'Is there enough silence in your day to hear God?' The honest answer was no. My days were a barrage of noise. Wall to wall meetings were crammed into the diary, friends and family filled days off and any other spare time was spent staring at a screen. My phone was the first thing I checked when I woke and the last before I slept – any time it buzzed in between, I was available. I might have been receptive to a lot of people, but I was in airplane mode when it came to listening to God. I finally decided to have another go at silence, this time just for a day.

I headed to a friend's house that I knew would be empty. I decided to cut the umbilical cord of phone signal and sit there until I heard God – or went crazy. At first my mind wandered all over the place. After some time, however, something odd began to happen. I suddenly began to notice emotions in myself I hadn't realised were there: anger, jealousy, envy, bitterness, fear and insecurity. I was shocked. I realised these emotions were linked with things that I'd done – being cruel to someone, acting selfishly, or refusing to forgive someone who'd hurt me. Taken aback, I began to repent of the things God brought to mind. How had all of this been there without me noticing? It was an uncomfortable experience. Towards the end of my time in the house a few verses from the Bible, ones that have always been foundational to me, came to mind. It was as if God was reminding me of who I was in him, repeating to me things I thought I knew but had forgotten.

The day felt like the spiritual equivalent of colonic irrigation! During space and time alone with God I was cleaned out. Things I'd been too busy to notice I was carrying were dealt with. Of course my mind wandered, I got distracted and I was bored at times, but it was more than worth it because by the time the day finished, I had heard God. I had a sense of his love, his steadfast kindness underpinning all my frantic rushing around – a little like stopping and putting your feet on the bottom of the swimming pool when you've been desperately thrashing about trying to stay afloat. It was as if he said, 'Aha, you've finally stopped to listen …' and seized his opportunity. In the weeks that followed that day I experienced a wonderful closeness with him; I began to notice him whispering to me in ways I hadn't spotted before.

Sheer Silence

Don't miss the point here. Silence in itself is not holy. If it were, the soundless vacuum that fills a room after Mike attempts a joke would be the holiest on earth.[7] God's voice is not literally a whisper. The point is, rather, that our lives are lived with a permanent background hum of activity – both physical and mental. Henri Nouwen once compared the mind to a banana tree full of monkeys jumping up and down. We are rarely still either on the outside or on the inside.

Yet it is in this stillness of heart and this quietening of our souls that we encounter God. The NRSV translates God's 'gentle whisper' as 'a sound of sheer silence' (1 Kings 19:12). Picture the prophet, alone in his cave, meeting with God in the utter silence.

There is tremendous value in cultivating a stillness of heart before God. External silence isn't the point, but it can be very helpful. Paul tells us that we are to 'pray without ceasing' (1 Thess. 5:17, NRSV), but in our experience if we never 'cease' everything

---

7   Andy wrote this sentence.

else just to pray, we will never pray without ceasing. When was the last time you ceased everything else to be with God?

Are we desperate enough to stop? Thirsty enough to withdraw? We want to 'hear God speak' but do we want to hear him enough to pursue being alone with him? In the middle of hectic lives and busy diaries how willing are we to carve out 'caves' of our own? Where in your life and at what point in your day do you have just silence and God for company? God is waiting to meet with you there.

> 'Be still and know that I am God' (Ps. 46:10) isn't just a command; it's a promise

We're not suggesting that initially you block off a whole day, though you may want to work towards that. Perhaps to begin, think about starting with ten minutes every other day. Your 'cave' may be your bedroom, your car as you drive to work or the short walk home from school. It will take a while to turn this into a regular habit; it isn't easy, but the benefits are enormous. Alone time with God is needed for intimacy with him. If you keep it up you'll begin to experience him in ways you haven't known before. 'Be still, and know that I am God' (Ps. 46:10) isn't just a command; it's a promise.

Busy? There's Hope!

Being alone with God is essential. In the busyness of life, however, there will be seasons when we cannot always do this. What do we do then? There is a second practice – it doesn't contradict the first, it sits alongside it as an important way of connecting with God.

ANDY

At the time of writing I have a busy job. Beth and I have a two-year-old, a one-year-old and a Mike. As you might imagine there isn't much time for silence and solitude. I schedule in retreat days, and plan moments of being alone with God each day, but regularly popping off for hours isn't realistic. During a day off I once suggested to Beth that she could continue to look after the kids whilst I go and pray. She was already exhausted and replied that if I did she'd really give me something to pray about! I have been trying to figure out how to be near to God when life is unavoidably full.

I had a breakthrough when I came across a book called *The Practice of the Presence of God*. It's written by a sixteenth century Carmelite monk called Brother Lawrence.[8] I liked it because it was simple and full of common sense spirituality. Brother Lawrence was a monk who learned to connect with God whilst he was washing the pots and pans. He had one simple lesson to teach: with just a little practise, it is possible to experience God's presence anywhere. This was a big encouragement to me – so often we think we can only meet with God when we are doing

---

8   Yes, Andy reads books by sixteenth century Carmelite monks. He's fun at parties.

something 'holy.' Brother Lawrence told me that I could meet with God when I was cleaning the car or changing a nappy – and I have to change a *lot* of those.[9]

Practising the Presence

There are no secret and complicated techniques when it comes to meeting with God. All that is needed is a determination to be with him and some straight-forward practices. Brother Lawrence argued it was a mistake to think we could only meet God when having a 'quiet time'. He said it's also possible to begin to experience life lived in God's presence. He offered a few simple tips on how to do this:

- Chat to God constantly, about anything and everything. Another word for this might be 'prayer'. This is simply knowing that God is keeping you company whatever you are up to, and talking to him as you might to a friend.

- Do all the normal things you need to get done – we usually think to be holy we have to stop all the normal things. However, this time practise doing them *for God*. A little like if you were cooking a meal for someone you love, you would be consciously doing it *for them*.

9   For clarification: Mike changes his own nappies.

Whatever you are doing, whether it's homework, cleaning, shopping or whatever, do it consciously *for God*. We can do this with *everything* and sometimes the more unpleasant the task, the greater the opportunity to do it as an act of love for him.

—   Keep going. We won't turn into Brother Lawrence after just two hours of this. Lawrence is pretty clear that a lot of the time we will forget and we'll make mistakes. When we do he tells us not to worry about it too much, and to start again. Keep having the goal of consciously doing everything 'for Jesus' in mind. If we do, he assures us, after some time we'll begin to experience a deeper intimacy with God.

These things sound so simple it can be tempting to dismiss them. We'd encourage you, however, to practise them. As we develop the habits of alone time with God, and the practise of the presence of God, the gentle whisper, heard fleetingly at first, will become the familiar voice of our Friend. We'll recognise it at church, in the supermarket or in the gym.

We Need Others

Cutting Ourselves Off

So, the Lord responded to Elijah's despair first with rest and food that would restore him physically and emotionally, and second with the intimacy of the gentle whisper that restored him spiritually.

There was, however, a third need that Elijah had. God had to restore him relationally.

After Carmel, Elijah left his servant in Beersheba and wandered *alone* in the wilderness. It was after a time of despairing isolation that he prayed 'I have had enough Lord,' and asked that he might die (1 Kings 19:4). So often when we hit rock bottom emotionally we do the same. We don't speak to the people we love the most. We cut ourselves off.

Why do we do this? It is one of Satan's oldest and most effective strategies. He usually waits till we are at our most vulnerable before suggesting isolation as a way to freedom. He suggests hiding as a means of protection. In the garden of Eden Adam and Eve ate the fruit from the tree and then they hid – not only from God in the trees, but also from each other behind fig leaves. They thought that hiding would solve the problem, but it made things worse. In wandering alone Elijah had just spent a day listening to his fears and being consumed by his thoughts, with no one to speak truth to him. Don't miss the fact that Jezebel sent him a threatening message – if she really thought she could harm him she probably would have just sent an assassin. She was playing mind games, trying to induce fear. The problem was Elijah had no one to talk it through with.

If Elijah's story teaches us the importance of being alone with God, it also teaches us the danger of being apart from people

Oh that we would learn the lesson and make sure that at the toughest times in our lives we are surrounded by those who love us! If Elijah's story teaches us the importance of being alone with God, it also teaches us the danger of being apart from people. Both matter. To reference Dietrich Bonhoeffer in his book *Life Together:* 'Let the one who cannot be alone beware of community … Let the one who is not in community beware of being alone.'[10] God knew Elijah needed others – even if Elijah couldn't see it himself.

The Gift of Elisha

Having heard the gentle whisper, Elijah stood at the entrance to the cave and the Lord asked him again, 'What are you doing here, Elijah?' Elijah repeated his miserable tale: he has been zealous for God, the people are hunting down and killing the Lord's prophets and now he – Elijah – is *the only one left.* At this point the Lord has a surprise for Elijah. We paraphrase: 'Hmmm … Elijah you know you've mentioned repeatedly you're the only one left. Actually, that's not *quite* true. This may come as a shock but there are actually *seven thousand others* who haven't worshipped Baal' (1 Kings 19:18).

This begs the question – why didn't the Lord mention this earlier? It's a little like believing that you are an only child for years only to find out your parents had five other children! We suspect if God had told Elijah any earlier of the seven thousand others,

10   Dietrich Bonhoeffer, *Life Together*, (Publisher, Harper & Row) 1954.

Elijah would have relied on them and not on God. God wants to lead each of us to a place where we rest ultimately on him – but the journey doesn't stop here. Then, not as a substitute to this relationship but *in addition to it,* God gives us others.

For Elijah, the most precious of the seven thousand others became Elisha. On God's orders he headed straight off Mount Horeb to anoint Elisha as his successor. The two were then inseparable until Elijah was taken up to heaven. When they were finally parted Elisha did not cry out, 'My colleague! My colleague!' or even, 'My mentor! My mentor!' but 'My father! My father!' (2 Kings 2:12). In the time they had been together they had formed a deep friendship.

Many of us make the mistake of settling for trying to follow God, or live life, alone. Of course, we don't completely cut ourselves off, but very few people ever get to really see our pain or share our joy. When we do this we are missing out! It can be tempting to say to ourselves: 'God is all I need.' The problem is, God disagrees with us – he knows we need others. One of the wisest things we can do as followers of Jesus is invest ourselves in deep, life-giving relationships with others going in the same direction. These people are precious gifts to us; they will enrich our lives, make us human and beckon us onwards in our journey with God. It is to the mysteries, the gifts and the challenges of friendships that our next lifeline speaks.

Read Elijah's Lifeline for Yourself

Elijah's story runs from 1 Kings 17 to 2 Kings 2. The key events include:

- Elijah and the widow at Zarephath, 1 Kings 17:7-24
- Elijah on Mount Carmel, 1 Kings 18:16-46
- Elijah on Mount Horeb, 1 Kings 19:1-18
- The call of Elisha, 1 Kings 19:19-21
- Naboth's vineyard, 1 Kings 21
- Elijah is taken to heaven, 2 Kings 2:1-18

It was prophesied that Elijah would return before 'the day of the Lord' came (Mal. 4:5-6). Jesus announced that this was fulfilled through John the Baptist (Matt. 11:12-14). Elijah also appeared and talked with Jesus at the Transfiguration (Matt. 17:3).

Group Questions

1. Can you recall times when you have been on a spiritual mountain top one day and a valley the next? How did that make you feel? Confused? Frightened? Despairing?
2. In your own life, have you noticed the connection between physical and emotional exhaustion on one hand, and spiritual dryness and lethargy on the other?
3. How hard do you find it to 'be still and know that he is God'? What practices could you introduce into your life to help you to listen to his 'gentle whisper'?

4. To what extent do you find it true that when you isolate yourself you feel low and when you feel low you isolate yourself?

5. Can you recall a time when you have heard God's gentle whisper and it has strengthened you?

6. Do you have 'Elishas' in your life who will stand with you, speak truth to you, bear burdens with you and love you?

CHAPTER 3

THE SECRETS OF FRIENDSHIP: LESSONS FROM THE LIFE OF RUTH

Greater love has no one than this: to lay down one's life for one's friends.

John 15:13

Splendid Isolation

---------------- ANDY ----------------

Some years ago I did a placement as a chaplain at a local hospital. I was somewhat shocked by the experience. A hospital is like 'humanity concentrated'. A giant petri dish of human beings, many of whom are at their most vulnerable, desperate and bewildered. Within five minutes one can walk from the maternity ward to the mortuary: quite literally from life to death. The highs of hope and recovery exist alongside the lows of failed treatment and deterioration. One meets both rejoicing relatives and sorrowful, empty-eyed friends. It is a place where people of all ages, ethnicities and religions co-exist bedside by bedside. A place that seems to have boiled off the 'everyday' parts of life, leaving behind an essence of humanity at its sharpest: birth, the fight for life and death.

My time was spent wandering around the lino-floored wards chatting with patients. I would always approach a person's bed feeling like I was intruding. It didn't seem right to be there to witness a stranger's total vulnerability. They were often unable to move, lying down; bodies wrapped in flimsy hospital gowns. These conversations became a window into people's lives.

The elderly would talk about their health problems, their hopes for recovery and, on more than one occasion, their wish to die. Yet the subject that they kept returning to was their relationships. I sat as people reminisced about their partners long-since dead, or shamelessly boasted about the achievements of their children. With remarkable regularity their eyes would wander to the clock on the wall, checking how many hours it was till the wards were opened to outside visitors. They clung to these promised visits like the drowning cling to lifeboats, talking about them for weeks in advance and days afterwards.

For all the physical suffering I saw during that time it was the loneliness that disturbed me the most. For some, hospital was a place where relationships deepened; they had bedsides full of visitors and more grapes than they knew what to do with. For others, however, in hospital the absence of these relationships became even more apparent. Conversations with these people revealed not just a bedside devoid of a visitor, but often a life lived in splendid isolation. One lady told me that in the twenty-eight years since her husband had died she had had few visitors to her home. In her words, 'I read a lot of books.' For many, this had been adjusted to as 'normal'. It was just the way the world was.

As I walked home at the end of each day I'd chat to God, wrestling through how He could 'sit idly by' whilst people shrank into tiny cocoons of existence far removed from each other. I know, of course, that in the end it's our society, not God's neglect, that has bred this loneliness, but I still asked the question.

During those weeks I was exposed to humanity at its most raw. I realised on a deeper level that we are, in our core, relational beings. When the all-consuming gadgets, the endless entertainment and the packed diaries are stripped away we are revealed to be people who long deeply to be connected with others. The obvious needs of the hospital patients revealed the innate needs of all human beings – the need for comfort, reassurance and friendship. Though most of us are able to hide it better, these needs exist in the hearts of everyone we meet.

Our Great Poverty

Loneliness comes in many shapes and sizes.

It may be an elderly hospital patient but it is just as likely to be the young parent, at home with the kids but with no chance to meet their own emotional needs. It could be the woman trying to get more and more followers on social media, but who in doing so is becoming less and less herself. It could be the man at the centre of the dance floor, hoping the flamboyant moves mask his sense of inadequacy. It might be the experienced manager, in charge of a lot of people but with no one to share the burden.

Loneliness isn't necessarily about being alone. It's possible to spend days without seeing people and be perfectly content. Equally, it's possible to be lonely in the midst of a crowd, a marriage, an office, a classroom or a church.

We were created with a need to be significant – first of all to God, but then equally, significant to each other. We need to know that we matter to someone. Loneliness is that feeling that we *don't*. It is the experience of being unwanted, unloved and uncared for. Mother Teresa once said that the greatest poverty she had ever encountered could be found in the most prosperous parts of the world: a poverty of loneliness. It is about a lack of connectedness: the feeling that no one really knows us, that if we weren't there, no one would really miss us.

We were created with a need to be significant – first of all to God, but then equally, significant to each other

We have both had seasons of loneliness in our lives. In our conversations with others we've also discovered that we aren't the only ones! So many at school, at university and in leadership have quietly confessed to us that they are leading lonely lives that it no longer shocks us. This is the world we live in. There have never been more of us on the planet; many live in cities where there are people all around; we have leisure options our parents could not even dream of; social media means we can instantly communicate our opinions to the rest of the world; yet we are suffering from an epidemic of loneliness.

Our society is full of advice about romantic relationships, but when it comes to friendship we're often left to make things up as we go along – with mixed results!

In the Bible true friendship is exalted as a big deal. God's heart is that we might have deep and fulfilling friendships with others and he provides guides as to how this might look. One of the greatest examples we have is a lady called Ruth. Before we look at her story, however, we want to set it in the context of the wider lessons the Scripture teaches on friendship.

There are two we will draw out:

The First 'Not Good'

Have you ever wondered why loneliness seems unnatural? Why it strikes us as so wrong?

In Genesis 1 we read that God created the world and the human race in six days. He took great satisfaction in his work and stood back to admire it. Seven times we are told that God saw that creation was 'good'. In the middle of all this goodness, however, God suddenly found something that was not good: 'The LORD God said, "It is not good for the man to be alone. I will make a helper suitable for him"' (Gen. 2:18). The first 'not good' of the Bible is to do with aloneness.

In the first instance this is about marriage, but it's about more than that – it's about the commodity that every great marriage is based on: friendship. God wasn't simply saying that Adam needed Eve. He was saying people need each other. We weren't designed to exist in isolation, this is why loneliness feels so wrong. God's first 'not good' was *before* sin entered the world, when everything was perfect. At this stage Adam would have been able to enjoy an unbroken, loving relationship with God. It is not uncommon for us to think, 'all I need is God.' Perhaps surprisingly, *God doesn't agree with this statement.* He knows we need friends.[11]

The 'Solution' to Loneliness

Have you ever checked how many 'friends', 'followers', or 'likes' you have on social media compared with somebody else?

No?

Sure. We haven't either ….[12]

One of the great myths of our time is that it is possible to have hundreds of close friends. Social media lends strength to this illusion. It allows us to feel connected to people we haven't met in years, if at all. This can be a great way of keeping in touch,

---

11   Tim Keller makes this point in *The Meaning of Marriage* (Hodder & Stoughton, 2011) 110-111.

12   And Andy would prefer it if you didn't check how many he has compared with Mike.

but it's a big mistake to think – as many of us do – the higher the 'friend' count, the lower the loneliness level. It is possible to have more followers than anyone else we know, and yet be far lonelier.

Proverbs 18:24 says, 'Some friends play at friendship but a true friend sticks closer than one's nearest kin' (NRSV). 'Playing at friendship' is having a lot of surface level relationships with others. It can be a good thing, but it won't deal with loneliness. For that, we need friends that stick close. We often think that popularity is the antidote to loneliness; if we can just get more people to 'like' us we won't feel so alone. The Bible shows this is not true. It is not

The solution to loneliness is not popularity with the masses; it is real intimacy with a few

the *quantity* of relationships that make the difference; it is the *quality*. The solution to loneliness is not popularity with the masses; it is real intimacy with a few.

It is only possible to sustain a small number of deep friendships. In the Bible we see the friendships of Moses and Joshua, David and Jonathan, Ruth and Naomi and Paul and Timothy. Even Jesus – the Son of God himself – only ever had a small group of friends. He spent time with crowds. He had dinner at people's houses and went to weddings and parties. But it seems that he always gravitated away from the masses to spend time with the twelve disciples. These were his close-knit friends. Even within the twelve he was especially close to just three, Peter, James and John. Others, such as Thaddaeus, barely get a mention.[13] The principles we'll be looking at in this chapter don't apply to every relationship. They relate to those few close friends.

Think quality, not quantity!

Decision on a Dirt Track

When we open the book of Ruth we are transported back over three thousand years. Imagine the book as a film. As the opening music plays you are given a summary of the backstory: When famine swept the land of Israel many left to find sanctuary in neighbouring lands. Among them were Elimelech, Naomi and their two sons. They settled down and the sons married, but soon first Elimelech then both his boys died. Devastated and consumed with bitterness, Naomi decided to return home …

The first scene of the film zooms in on a dirt track, far outside the safety of the city. Under the Middle Eastern sun Ruth, Orpah and their mother-in-law Naomi stand facing one another. Naomi makes a speech she has clearly been building up to for weeks: 'Then Naomi said to her two daughters-in-law, "Go back, each of you, to your mother's home. May the LORD show you kindness, as you have shown kindness to your dead husbands and to me. May the LORD grant that each of you will find rest in the home of another husband"' (Ruth 1:8-9).

Ruth and Orpah start to weep as Naomi kisses them goodbye. They refuse to leave her, insisting, 'We will go back with you to

---

13   Yes, Thaddaeus was a disciple. We were surprised too.

your people' (v. 10). We imagine Naomi shaking her head wearily; she must have known this would be difficult. She insists they leave her. She explains that they have no hope of finding another husband where she is going, saying, 'As hard as this is for you, it's harder for me; God has turned against me.' The two young women begin to cry again. Then Orpah, seeing that Naomi's mind is made up, kisses her goodbye. The Scripture tells us, however, 'Ruth clung to her' (v. 14).[14]

Ruth then makes a speech of her own. Bear in mind that Ruth is not someone historians would consider significant. She wasn't a leader, a prophet or a queen. She wasn't even Jewish. And yet three thousand years after she lived, this young Moabite woman is cheering us on as we follow God. Her life is still speaking. It is because of these words, this decision on a dirt track.

'But Ruth replied, "Don't urge me to leave you or to turn back from you. Where you go I will go, and where you stay I will stay. Your people will be my people and your God my God. Where you die I will die, and there I will be buried. May the LORD deal with me, be it ever so severely, if even death separates you and me"' (vv. 16-17).

Being Ruth

Ruth makes a promise to Naomi in this moment: she isn't going anywhere. This is a remarkable act of courage and selflessness, but above all it's an act of friendship. At this point we would love to

---

14   We think this is the only recorded incident in history of someone clinging to their *mother-in-law.*

move into writing a chapter titled, 'Finding Your Ruth – Getting the Best Friends for Yourself.'

Step One: Move to a foreign land.
Step Two: Endure a series of tragic events.
Step Three: (To test their loyalty) attempt to abandon your two remaining companions on the side of the motorway.

Unfortunately, we're not sure that's how it works. The Bible seems to teach repeatedly that the way to self-fulfilment is self-sacrifice; the way to find your life is to *lose it*. We address the loneliness many of us experience not, as we might imagine, by figuring out how to *attract* lots of friends. It begins with learning how to *be* friends to others. This chapter is not about how to 'get a Ruth' it's about how to '*be* a Ruth' to someone else. Having this approach is the only way we'll ever develop genuine deep friendships.

In the speech that Ruth makes to Naomi we discover a pattern for all great friendships: *I will go with you; I will stay with you; I will die with you.*

'I Will Go With You'

The two of us once toured Canada. It's a big country and we were often driving for six to seven hours a day. Andy is an introvert and not a fan of small talk. We found ourselves sitting in the back of the car either side of a lady who was lovely, but with whom we had nothing in common. Unfortunately, she didn't feel the same way and wouldn't stop talking. After a couple of days of trying to be polite Andy was at breaking point. He did the only thing he could think of: he put on his headphones and pretended to be listening to music – for six hours. It worked. She talked to Mike instead. Mike is also an introvert; he just didn't have any headphones.

We can sit in a car, on a plane or at a meal with someone and realise within minutes that the next few hours may be some of the longest of our life. (Wedding receptions are often the nightmare scenario.) Without at least some common connection it's hard to maintain a conversation, let alone a friendship. One of the keys to friendship is a shared interest. This means that waking up one morning deciding that we are going to build a brilliant friendship, and then scrolling randomly through our contacts to find a 'victim' probably won't work. Great friendships are usually *discovered* rather than simply made by decision.

It was CS Lewis who pointed out friendship is always *about* something. Whilst lovers might stare longingly into each other's eyes for hours, friends don't. Instead it is as if we stand side-by-side looking at the same object. Both of us are captivated by it and we bond over that. We watch football together, we play video games, or we connect over a film. The best lovers do this as well of course; great friendship is the foundation of a great marriage. Lewis wrote: 'Friendship must be *about* something, even if it were only an enthusiasm for dominoes or white mice. Those who have nothing can share nothing; those who are going nowhere can have no fellow-travellers.' Friendships are built *on* something. They begin when we meet someone of whom we say, "Oh, you like [insert white mice equivalent]. Me too!"

Walking Together

The point we are making is this: friendship is about journeying somewhere with someone. At its simplest this is 'going to' a shared interest. At its deepest it is about having a shared *purpose*. Another way of answering the question, 'What am I called to in life?' is to ask a different one, 'Who am I called to go with?' Ruth's vow to go with Naomi was a declaration of 'me too!' '*You are going on an adventure to rebuild your life – me too, I'm going with you.*' They didn't sit by the side of the road 'being friends', they set out on a make-or-break venture, and they had a common purpose, a shared mission.

Tim Keller makes the point that the best friendships develop where there is a combination of natural and supernatural interest.[15] The two of us have been friends for more than a decade. We are different in age (by about thirty years), in dress sense (Andy has one) and in temperament (one of us is a robotic Englishman, the other an excitable Greek). However, we would say that we have found our closest friend in the other. Mike was the best man at Andy's wedding. Andy was the best man when Mike ate an entire hog roast. One of the reasons for this is that we share natural interests – we enjoy the same TV shows and books, we compete at sport, we follow current affairs. Another foundational reason, though, is that we are called to serve Jesus *together*. We have a common desire to spend ourselves in the advancement of his kingdom; we know that we are called to do this jointly, as a team. When the form or shape of the ministry changes, the fact that we

---

15   Keller makes this point in his excellent chapter on marriage and friendship (The *Meaning of Marriage*, 113-117), with reference to CS Lewis' *The Four Loves* (New York: Mariner Books, 1971), chapter 4.

will be doing it together won't. Come what may, we are going on an adventure with Jesus. This common goal is a tremendous source of strength to both of us.

These types of friendships are rare and they can't be forced. They can be nurtured but initially they are something we discover. Sometimes we journey with people for a season that naturally comes to a close. There are, however, a handful of people God will put in our lives, to whom we are called for the long haul.

Who is travelling in the same direction as you?

I Will Stay with You

It can be hard to miss what a remarkable statement Ruth made when she vowed, 'I will stay with you.' There were a number of reasons why Ruth might have walked away from this relationship:

1. Naomi told her to! She was ordering her daughters-in-law to go back to their homes.
2. Naomi was a bitter old woman. She later changed her name from 'Naomi' which means 'pleasant,' to 'Mara' which means 'bitter' (Ruth 1:20). Imagine the dinner conversation: *'So, Bitter, how has your day been?'*
3. Ruth's prospects of finding a new husband were slim to none. She was leaving her own people and homeland and would be a second-class citizen in Israel. Of course, God had other plans (see the rest of the story) but Ruth wasn't to know that.

One thing is clear: Ruth wasn't sticking around because there was something in it for her. True friends are the people who walk in

True friends are the people who walk in when everyone else is walking out

when everyone else is walking out. This is where a few quality relationships are far better than lots of skin-deep ones. We might have lots of admirers on social media or at the office, but the test of friendship is, will they stay when there is nothing left to admire? Who are the people who, if life went wrong – if they lost their job, marriage, health, looks or money – we would still be there for? These are the people we are friends to.

Master Samwise Gamgee

Andy is a fan of *The Lord of the Rings*. You may have seen the films or read the books. If not – spoiler alert! They are about a hobbit called Frodo. He has to throw an evil ring in a big volcano (it just takes him twelve hours of film/three whole books, to get there).

In the first film – *The Fellowship of the Ring* – the story is about Frodo and his companions journeying to Mount Doom. There comes a point where one of the fellowship turns on Frodo and tries to steal the ring. In this moment, Frodo realises how evil the ring is. He recognises it may corrupt his friends and decides to go on alone.

During a battle with some orcs Frodo seizes his opportunity to slip away. He races to a nearby river, pushes a canoe into the water and begins to paddle. He is fleeing not just from his enemies, but also from his friends. Frodo hasn't accounted, however, for the steadfastness of his closest companion – Samwise Gamgee. Sam realises what Frodo is up to and rushes after him. By the time he bursts through the trees Frodo is already some distance from shore, rowing away.

Sam cries out in anguish, 'Not alone Frodo. Mr. Frodo!'

Frodo, with tears in his eyes, keeps paddling. He whispers to himself, 'No, Sam.'

Sam looks at the water, then at the boat. He launches himself into the water. Frodo, hearing the splash and looking behind, yells, 'Go back, Sam.'

Sam keeps wading.

'I'm going to Mordor alone,' cries Frodo.

'Of course you are … and I'm coming with you,' replies Sam as he splashes hopelessly towards the boat.

'You can't swim!' Frodo shouts.

Sam begins to go under; he is spluttering and coughing. Frodo, frightened now, stands up in the boat, 'Sam!'

Sam begins to drown. He sinks beneath the surface of the water, hands outstretched towards Frodo. It looks as if Sam is going to die. Suddenly Frodo's hand plunges into the water and grabs Sam. He pulls the bedraggled, half-drowned hobbit into the boat. Frodo and Sam look at each other, both out of breath, with tears and water streaming down their faces.

'I made a promise Mr. Frodo … a promise,' says Sam with fierce passion, '"Don't you leave him, Samwise Gamgee." And I don't mean to … I don't mean to.'

As friends, our role is to be a Sam. This is not always easy. Often when people we love are struggling – say with an eating disorder, anxiety, depression, a divorce, redundancy, a bereavement – they attempt to go it alone. They, like Frodo, run even from their friends. One reason for this is self-protection; we don't like being exposed; we don't want our shame or weakness to be seen. Another reason is to attempt to protect others - we don't want to 'burden them' with our issues.

Naomi attempts to do this with her daughters-in-law. She pushes them away. Ruth's response is much like Sam's: 'Where on earth do you think you are going without me?' Don't hear what we are not saying – our job is not to *fix* our friends.

We can sometimes end up damaged or making the situation worse by trying to take on that which only God can heal. If a friend is struggling with self-harm, addiction or depression, it is not within our power to 'solve' that for them. Sam could not take the ring from Frodo. However, he *could* refuse to abandon him. He *could* insist on going with him on the journey. Ruth did not say to Naomi, 'I will solve your problems Naomi, I'll sort your life out.' She said something far simpler, but nevertheless very powerful, 'In the midst of all your problems, I'll stay with you.'

The Power of Commitment

All this is another way of saying that in any great friendship there has to be commitment. We see this in another meaningful friendship in the Bible: David and Jonathan. This was a relationship that might have been defined by rivalry. Jonathan was the next in line for the throne; David was the rising star in the military. Instead, it became defined by a mutual commitment. The Biblical word is 'covenant.' We read: 'Jonathan made a covenant with David because he loved him as himself. Jonathan took off the robe he was wearing and gave it to David, along with his tunic, and even his sword, his bow and his belt' (1 Sam. 18:3-4).

The marriage covenant is unique before God. However, in our fickle and lonely world there is also a desperate need for deep, lasting, committed friendships. Jonathan and David became committed friends, and that allowed for real openness. In the handing over of his weapons Jonathan was making a statement to David: it was one of vulnerability. 'David – if you choose to, you can attack me.'

ANDY

I was once sitting with a friend in a bar; his girlfriend had just broken up with him. I attempted to comfort him but after a time he waved it off. He told me, 'I'll be okay Andy, don't worry about me.' Then he explained his approach to relationships: 'I see myself as a castle. Sometimes I let people behind the outer wall. Sometimes I let people behind the inner wall. But no one ever gets into the keep.' I remember understanding exactly what he meant. Until Jesus had begun to work in my heart I too had put up very strong walls. If I was hurting I made sure no one saw it. I learnt that the best way to stop myself from being wounded was to limit how much of myself I 'gave away'. The trouble with this is if no one gets into 'the keep' then no one ever truly knows you. It is a lonely way to live. True friendship is giving the keys to your keep to another.

When mutual commitment doesn't exist, we usually feel that we need to put on a show. Our world treats relationships in the way we treat phone contracts. As long as the deal is a good one for us, we'll stay. The moment the costs of a friendship start to outweigh the benefits, we'll leave. The minute we spot a better deal elsewhere, we'll upgrade. The problem with this approach is that it breeds insecurity. We can end up thinking, 'I need to be a "good deal". I am really struggling at the moment, but I'd better look fun/smart/sexy at the party or they won't invite me back.'

> *When mutual commitment doesn't exist, we usually feel that we need to put on a show*

Commitment creates a safe space. A place where we can be ourselves, take off our masks and stop pretending without fear of being judged or rejected. When we are committed to other people it says to them, 'Even though I've just discovered you are [insert nightmare shame scenario] I'm not going anywhere. I'm a friend to *you*, not you "on a good day". I'm not in this because of what I can get out of it.'

On People's Worst Days

Friendships like this are rare. Jonathan's commitment to David extended to David's *worst* days. When Jonathan's father Saul began to see David as a threat he tried to murder him. At great cost to himself Jonathan stood up to Saul. He protected David numerous times and eventually, when he could no longer guarantee David's safety, Jonathan warned him to run. In a moving passage we read: 'they kissed each other and wept together – but David wept the most. Jonathan said to David, "Go in peace, for we have sworn friendship with each other in the name of the LORD"' (1 Sam. 20:41-42).

David then began a life in exile. At this point he was no longer a popular general. He was not someone who would be a strategic or politically useful friend. He was an outlaw – an enemy of the state. Jonathan could easily have had David killed; at the very least he could have cut ties with him. Instead he did the opposite.

Jonathan sought David out in the wilderness 'and helped him find strength in God. "Don't be afraid," he said. "My father Saul will not lay a hand on you. You will be king over Israel, and I will be second to you. Even my father Saul knows this." The two of them made a covenant before the LORD' (1 Sam. 23:16-18). Let us repeat: Jonathan was the crown prince; David was a fugitive. The political power and military might was all in Jonathan's hands. At this, David's lowest and most vulnerable point, Jonathan *renewed* the covenant with him. More than that, he insisted that David would be king in his place. Make no mistake; Jonathan was neither weak, nor a doormat. He was a popular, strong and hugely capable leader in his own right. But he knew what it was to be a friend.

The test of the friendship we show to others is how we behave at their lowest moments. At points like this most people do not need advice; they need to know they are loved and accepted. They need to know that we see them at their worst – we see their porn addiction, or their mood swings, or their wounded broken hearts, and we are staying anyway. This level of friendship doesn't develop over night; it takes

> *The test of the friendship we show to others is how we behave at their lowest moments*

years. Who are those who, when they face difficult times, will find us swimming towards their boat, renewing our covenant and vowing to stay?

Betrayed With a Kiss

It can be hard to read a chapter about 'being a Ruth' if we have been badly bruised in a friendship. This is sometimes the sad result of living in a sinful world. We are broken and we will hurt others, and vice versa.

The great risk in opening ourselves up to others is, of course, that we are vulnerable to being wounded by them. There are few things more painful. If you have experienced this you are not alone. David also knew what it was like. In Psalm 55:12-14 he writes: 'If an enemy were insulting me, I could endure it; if a foe were rising against me, I could hide. But it is you, a man like myself, my companion, my close friend, with whom I once enjoyed sweet fellowship at the house of God.' David would rather have an enemy attack him, than a friend betraying him.

Jesus also knew this type of pain. He allowed Judas Iscariot into his inner circle and Judas literally sold him out. Jesus was betrayed with a kiss; sent to his death by someone he loved. Even the best friendships can go wrong. To love at all is to risk being hurt.

Unfortunately, the only way we can prevent any future pain is to put the armour on, put the walls up, and not let anyone inside the keep. Whilst this may sound appealing, it is a fast-track to loneliness. We may be emotionally 'safe', but we will never be close to anyone. We may numb ourselves to the hurt relationships can bring, but we also numb ourselves to the joy and the life they give us.

If we have been hurt – and both of us have personally known this type of pain – a better response than sealing ourselves off is to be wise about whom we trust ourselves to. It is to be brave enough to, perhaps slowly at first, try again. It has been our experience that whilst we receive much hurt from relationships, we also receive much of our healing through them. They are worth the risk.

I Will Die with You!

We cannot prove this from the text, but we suspect Ruth attended a drama school in Moab. She certainly knew how to build a speech to a crescendo …

I will go with you.

I will stay with you!

I WILL DIE WITH YOU!

By the time Ruth was declaring she was going to be buried in the same grave as her, Naomi had probably gotten the point. Still, the language was appropriate. Making a commitment is the easy part – keeping it is the hard part. When the rubber hit the dirt track, for Ruth, this act was a dying to self.

'Me First' to 'You First'

Know that your few great friendships will cost you dearly – time, money, emotional energy, patience and much more. Jesus said, 'My command is this: Love each other as I have loved you. Greater love has no one than this: to lay down one's life for one's friends' (John 15:12-13). Any great friendship is an exercise in dying to self. Our culture tends to teach that the ultimate expression of love is sex. The Bible shows us that the ultimate expression of love is not sex but sacrifice.

These sacrifices outwork themselves in all sorts of ways.

Most of us want to be the star. But Paul encourages the church in Rome to 'love from the centre of who you are; don't fake it … Be good friends who love deeply; practice playing second fiddle' (Rom. 12:9-10, THE MESSAGE). We've heard that 'second fiddle' is one of the hardest roles in the orchestra. You are not in the limelight, in fact you are out of it, but your role is essential; it's to add texture to the music, to make sure whoever is playing 'first fiddle' is made to look and sound good. Friends do this for each other. They put their own ambitions, dreams and hopes to one side in order to cheer the other on. Their goal is that the other person becomes the best that they can be.

Most of us don't want to forgive when we are hurt, but great friendships are made up of great forgivers. Any authentic relationship that lasts longer than a few weeks will involve occasional arguments. When these happen the easy option is to walk away, or hold on to a grudge. However, when we deal with these moments well – we talk it out, forgive, and let go – the friendship is strengthened, not weakened, as a result. Forgiveness is never easy, it involves a 'dying to self', but it comes with the territory in quality friendships.

Iron Sharpens Iron

Another way of sacrificing for our friends is learning to 'speak the truth in love'. In other words, learning to say hard things because we care about the other person. We often avoid having difficult conversations with each other because we don't want to risk the relationship or hurt the person. However, *good* friends will speak truth into our lives. They defend us behind our backs, and tell us what they really think to our faces! When we see our friends going off down a destructive path or selling themselves short, it's our job to say something. We aren't suggesting you start texting some 'home truths' to your close friends. But good signs it might be time to speak up are:

a.   You don't really want to, but

b.   You care about the person too much to keep your mouth shut.

Proverbs 27:6 tells us, 'Wounds from a friend can be trusted.' Friends challenge one another because they care, and they want to see the other thrive. If you have a friend who tells you the truth, they are worth their weight in gold.

— ANDY —

Not long after I graduated Mike and I were travelling somewhere. As we drove I made a throw away, dismissive comment about someone. We continued driving for a while in silence and it dawned on me that what I'd said had been unbelievably big-headed. It was reflective of a pattern I'd begun to notice. I turned to Mike and said, 'Hey mate, I think in the last year or so I may have become quite proud.' He paused for a minute, and then said kindly but firmly, 'Yes Andy, I've been meaning to talk to you about that.' We went on to have quite a chat. Ouch!

On another occasion I was preaching at a university. Mike came along to support me. The talk was followed by a question and answer session from the students. It was the first of a series and I was keen to get it right so afterwards I asked Mike for feedback. He told me, 'You did a great job in the talk. Well done!' Then he paused, and went on to say, 'In the Q&A you came across like a bit of an idiot.' He then did an exaggerated impression of me

answering questions! At that moment I really felt like an idiot.
I'm making two points here:

1. Mike can be a moron.
2. I thank God for him. There is someone in my life who cares
    about me enough to confront me. He does it because he is
    on my side. He will tell me when I'm doing well, but he'll
    also challenge me to grow. I know I don't need to be defensive;
    I know we are a team.[16]

Another Proverb reads, 'As iron sharpens iron, so one person
sharpens another' (Prov. 27:17). In a great friendship, as we
challenge and spur one another on, we become greater than the
sum of our parts.

Ruth died to herself. She sacrificed the comfortable, safe option
of returning to her own people, and instead headed off with Naomi
into an uncertain future. The rest of the book of Ruth shows
Naomi doing the same for
Ruth. She became devoted
to Ruth's welfare, doing everything she could to help her find
another husband, something
which in that culture was the
same as securing a future.

> *To be a great
> friend to someone
> is to put them
> before ourselves*

To be a great friend to
someone is to put them before

---

16   For integrity's sake Andy should probably mention that he has also chal-
lenged Mike many times. Unfortunately his motives have not always been as pure
– it has often just been about revenge.

ourselves. This may mean helping them succeed, it may mean weeping with them in their failures, it will mean forgiveness and it will mean sometimes speaking the truth in love.

Who are we willing to do this for?

The Greatest Friend

Going with someone, staying with someone and dying with someone – it sounds like a big ask!

Our hope in living this out rests not on Ruth but on her great-great-great-grandson, Jesus.[17] He teaches us to love in a very specific way: 'Love each other as I have loved you' (John 15:12). Herein lies the true secret to being a Ruth to someone else. In most relationships we tend to love people in the way *they* love us:

- If they say something nice to us, we compliment *them* in return.
- If they do the washing up for us, we do it for *them*.
- If they buy us a birthday present, we buy *them* a birthday present (of a similar monetary value).

On a good day we love someone the way *they* love us.

This, however, is not how Jesus teaches us to love.

We are to love each other as *he* has loved us.

---

17   And a few more 'greats' – Ruth was great-grandma to king David, from whom Jesus was descended.

This is a radical shift. We are to love others not how we think they deserve to be loved, but *how we have been loved by Jesus, the greatest of friends.* Jesus has invited us to go with him on the ultimate adventure – to rebuild the world and restore our lives along the way. Jesus has made a covenant with us, sealed with his blood. He committed himself to us at our worst and lowest moment, when we were full of sin and far from him. He is staying. And Jesus has died for us. He gave his life that we might find eternal life.

Our role as friends is not to love our friends in the way they love us back. It is to love them as Jesus has loved us. If we can't love our friends like this, what hope have we of loving the rest of the world?

Our Friendships can Change the World

Jesus said: 'A new command I give you: Love one another. As I have loved you, so you must love one another. By this everyone will know that you are my disciples, if you love one another' (John 13:34-35). In other words, if we love each other – in the way Jesus has loved us – the world will see that we know the Son of God.

Think about that.

The master plan for evangelism was not 'convert some famous people and get them to tell others about me'. Nor was it 'have the best music and light show in town'. It wasn't even 'become really smart and out-argue people'. It was *love each other; in the way I've loved you.*

We cannot think of a better way to display the love of God than through churches full of friends like these. Wouldn't that look remarkable to the people visiting? Isn't that a family you would want to join? One of the most powerful things we can do to deal with the loneliness we are facing and that our world is facing is this: decide to be a Ruth.

Read Ruth's Lifeline for Yourself

Ruth's story is told in the book of Ruth. We have concentrated on her decision to return to Israel with Naomi but they then had quite the adventure together. Some key events are:

- Ruth returns with Naomi, Ruth 1
- Ruth meets her future husband, Boaz, Ruth 2-3
- Ruth marries Boaz and they have Obed the grandfather of David, Ruth 4

Group questions

1. In what ways do you think social media actually results in us becoming more lonely and isolated?
2. Friendship involves risk and vulnerability. Do you agree? Can you name some of the risks and vulnerabilities in your own life?
3. How do you deal with the pain that comes when someone close hurts you or lets you down? How could or should you deal with it?

4. In what ways have you found healing through deep friendships?

5. What stops you from getting close to others?

6. 'I will die with you.' How did Jesus love the disciples? How are we to love one another in the same way? What does that look like?

CHAPTER 4

WHEN LIFE GOES WRONG: LESSONS FROM THE LIFE OF JOSEPH

And we know that in all things God works for the good of those who love him, who have been called according to his purpose.

Romans 8:28

--- ANDY ---

Three weeks ago I received a text: 'We're having a boy!'

I was away and my wife was having our 20-week scan. I punched the air and shouted with delight! I didn't care whether we had a boy or a girl; I was just excited to know! Beth had been under strict instructions to make contact the instant she knew the gender of the baby. I didn't want anyone knowing before I did. I paced around my room relishing the moment and began coming up with names. 'We've got a Josiah and a Judah, should we go for another J …?'

Then my phone buzzed again: 'They think there's a problem with the heart.'

I stood holding my phone and starring dumbly at the screen. 'What? That can't be true. It just can't be.'

Another text: 'Please pray.'

Those messages fired the starting gun on a desperate forty-eight hours. Beth and I were scared and confused. We already had two children and had never encountered a problem like this one. We were told we would need a further detailed scan with a specialist to find out if there really was a problem. Miraculously a space opened up the next day. Beth went with her mum, while I travelled home as quickly as I could.

The hospital appointment lasted hours; waiting to hear the outcome was agony. I ran through possible results in my head – my favourite being, Scenario A: This was all a terrible mistake and the second scan would prove it. Beth would be home soon and we'd go out to dinner to celebrate and give thanks to God. We would be laughing about this in a few days.

The time crawled by. Eventually Beth called. I leapt at the phone. Within seconds I knew: it wasn't Scenario A. Between sobs my wife told me that our unborn son had been diagnosed with a very rare heart condition. It affects one in ten thousand babies. There were lots of other things Beth said – to do with missing blood vessels, multiple surgeries and genetic disorders – but I couldn't take them in. I couldn't get past the words, 'very rare heart condition'.

Putting the phone down, I wept.

Twenty days later, Mike and I are revisiting this chapter. We wrote the first draft months ago. As you might well imagine, I am now reading it with new eyes.

Life: Harder Than We Expected

Many of us imagine life to be, if not easy, then at least straightforward. We've been conditioned to think like this. Growing up, we were repeatedly told we could 'be anything we wanted to be.' We were handed medals for just showing up at our school sports days. In the films and box sets we watch daily things always seem to come together. Everyone we follow on social media appears to have it all worked out. We hope, dream, wish and – crucially – *expect* things to fall into place for us too.

Yet in truth, life's journey is usually far harder than we anticipate. As a result, when it throws a punch, we are left reeling. Partly because of the blow itself, but also because of the shock of it all – this wasn't how it was meant to be! There are few things more painful than having hopes dashed and dreams wrecked. There are also few things more confusing. Where is God in all of this? I thought he was meant to be my Saviour? I thought he was meant to be in charge? I thought he was supposed to love me?

The place that we turn to for guidance is, as in all things, the Bible. Here we find that we are not alone in discovering that life can be hard. Jesus was abandoned and betrayed by his closest friends, before being tortured and executed. With the exception of

John, tradition tells us Jesus' remaining eleven apostles were martyred. The early church was a persecuted church. Things were no easier in the Old Testament. The prophets, leaders and people of Israel all faced testing times. Repeatedly, however, God called people to follow him *not away from* hardship but *through it.*

Most of us will find, at some point, life diverts horribly from the track we'd imagined it might take. We cannot see the way back, let alone the way ahead. Fortunately, at moments like these, there are those who can direct us because they have, in a sense, been there before us. This chapter is about one such guide: his name is Joseph.

The Story of Joseph

Joseph's story is one of our favourites in the Bible. It has everything: a family that could be a case study for a psychiatrists' conference, plot twists more farfetched than a soap opera, and an unbelievably happy ending. We'd encourage you to read the whole story for yourself – it can be found in Genesis 37-50 – but here follows our idiot's guide to the life of Joseph:

The Pampered Teenager

Joseph had ten older brothers. He was, by any account, spoilt. His brothers had to make do with hand-me-downs while Joseph, his father's favourite, wore tailor-made, designer clothes. To make matters worse he would tell tales about his brothers. All this meant that they, with justification, didn't like him very much – in fact they hated him!

As a teenager Joseph had a couple of dreams from God. At this point Joe comes across as fairly arrogant – yet God spoke to him. Let's just stop and consider that for a moment: Why did God speak to a pampered, proud seventeen year old? For the same reason that he is willing to speak to you and us. God loves us despite our faults.

Joe told his brothers about his dreams. His interpretation? That one day he would be standing tall while they bowed before him. He'd be in the centre with millions of Instagram followers, big brand sponsorship and his own fashion label. On hearing this news his ten older brothers did what any normal, self-respecting older brothers would do: they sold him into slavery.

Hitting Rock Bottom

Jacob – Joseph's father – was sold the lie that wild animals had killed Joseph. Meanwhile, the teenager was taken to Egypt and found himself enslaved to a guy called Mr Potiphar, a member of the Egyptian elite. All seemed to go reasonably well for a while, until one day when Mr Potiphar was away on business. Mrs Potiphar went into Joseph's room and invited him to 'make her acquaintance '. He refused, she got upset, he tried to leave, she grabbed his cloak, he escaped, but she claimed he had tried to rape her. The foreign slave had no chance. He was put in prison where he languished for years.

Eventually a baker and a cupbearer (in other words, a waiter) were put in the prison with him. They had worked for Pharaoh and both had dreams that they didn't understand. Joseph asked God what their dreams meant and interpreted them. For the cupbearer it was good news; for the baker not so much. The cupbearer was released, as Joseph had said he would be, and restored to his old job working for Pharaoh. The baker, however, was terminated. As the cupbearer was being released, Joseph begged him, 'Please don't forget me.' The cupbearer said, 'Sure thing Joe!', and promptly forgot him.

Raised Up

Years passed and eventually Pharaoh had a dream about fat cows and thin cows. No one could understand it. Then the cupbearer suddenly remembered the foreigner in prison who was good with dreams. Soon Joseph found himself standing in front of Pharaoh. In response to the king's request, Joe said, 'I don't interpret dreams – it's God who gives the interpretation – but I'll ask him for you!' God revealed the meaning and Joseph was able to prophesy seven years of economic growth followed by a great depression.

Pharaoh then promoted this foreign slave into the position of Prime Minister of Egypt! Overnight Joseph became the leader of the world's Super Power. He then oversaw the seven years of prosperity and made provision for the seven years of famine. It meant that when the shortages began Egypt had the reserves to survive. All the surrounding nations started to starve and people began to flock to Egypt for help.

Re-enter the brothers. With so many mouths to feed the family was in a terrible state, so the ten travelled from Canaan to beg for food. In an incredible twist, they found themselves in front of Joseph, but had no idea who he was. Cutting a long story short,

Joe eventually told them. They were shocked and terrified! Joseph forgave them and promised to look after them. The whole family travelled to Egypt and was reunited. Joseph died at a good old age surrounded by people he loved.

No Filter

It's possible to read Joseph's story as a tale of rags to riches: the miraculous transformation of the eleventh son of an Israelite farmer into the Prince of Egypt. A story of success, not failure, of life going right, not wrong. If we do this, though, we filter out the terrible pain and suffering that Joseph experienced on the way to fulfilling his God-given dreams. We've made light of it in our summary, but don't miss the horrendous trials Joseph had to endure: utter betrayal by his brothers. Thirteen dark years of slavery and wrongful imprisonment. Joseph knew more than most about life going wrong.

Were he to give a seminar titled 'When Life Goes Wrong' what would Joseph teach us? What advice would he pass on from his experience? We suspect the following four lessons would make an appearance.

Lesson One: God Is With You

Where is God?

The first question most of us ask when life goes wrong is 'God, where are you?' Our assumption is usually that if God is with us then

Our assumption is usually that if God is with us then nothing bad should happen to us. The Bible shows time and again that this assumption is wrong

nothing bad should happen to us. The Bible shows time and again that this assumption is wrong. Jesus – who actually *was* God With Us ('Emmanuel') – himself faced the cross. Isaiah, in the book that prophetically names Jesus 'Emmanuel', foretold of him: 'He was despised and rejected by mankind, a man of suffering, and familiar with pain' (Isa. 53:3). If Emmanuel was not immune from pain, we should not expect to be. God being with us does not prevent bad things from happening; he is not a good luck charm. And our suffering does not mean God has abandoned us – far from it!

God is With Us

When we ask, 'Where is God in Joseph's life?' the Bible gives us a remarkable answer. Joseph's tale accounts for ninety-three years of his long life, and as biblical stories goes it is pretty detailed. It takes thirteen chapters, or – in the NIV – 10,068 words to tell in full. These chapters add up to a grand total of 419 verses – that's a lot!

How many of these 419 verses tell us where God is?

Just two.

The first is when Joseph was a slave: 'the LORD was with Joseph so that he prospered' (Gen. 39:2).

The second is when Joseph was a prisoner: 'But while Joseph was there in prison, the LORD was with him; he showed him kindness and granted him favour' (vv. 20-21).

Let us repeat this point: throughout Joseph's ninety-three year story we are only explicitly told *twice* that God was with him. These are *not*, as we might expect, at the high-points of Joseph's life; not when he was a spoiled teenager or a powerful Prime Minister. Instead, they are during the loneliest and most painful seasons of his life. The first when he was a slave, the second when he was a prisoner.

This is astonishing. What does it tell us?

God wants to make the point: it is in our slavery, and in our prison, that *he is particularly near*. God's first response to our pain is not always to stop the cause of it – although we probably wish it were! God's initial reaction to Joe's jail sentence was not to break Joseph *out* of prison; instead, remarkably, God broke *into* the prison. He didn't instantly end Joe's jail term; he kept him company throughout it. It has been the experience of many that when we are suffering we discover that God is very close.

Close in the Darkness

In David's most famous psalm, he wrote, 'Even though I walk through the darkest valley, I will fear no evil, for you are with me; your rod and your staff, they comfort me' (Ps. 23:4). The same verse that speaks of the darkest valley, or the valley of the shadow

of death, speaks also of God being *with us*. This is God's initial
'solution' to our hurt – his companionship.

There's an old story that we love. It's about a father and son.
The son moves into a new bedroom in the attic. The first night he
is uncomfortable and scared – there are strange noises and it's unfa-
miliar. Eventually, to reassure him, his dad gives him a choice. He
can switch the main light on and keep it on all night. Or he can
switch the light off but have his dad stay with him in the room.
The boy goes for the second option. When it comes to comfort *he
would rather have his father's presence in the darkness than his absence
in the light.*

Our experience has been similar. We can endure almost any
pain when we know there are people who are in it with us, who
love us, who have our backs. How much more when we know the
one with us is our heavenly Father? Were we to ask Joseph, 'Did
God abandon you?' we know his answer would be, 'No way – I've
never known him closer than during those years in prison.'

God is in Control

If knowing God is close is essential, it's also important to know
he is in control. God is Love – he's near, but he is also Lord – he
oversees events. It's not that we are hopelessly lost at sea and happen
to have another desperate companion in the boat with us. It's that
the one with us holds the oceans in the palm of his hand. This
changes our perspective on everything.

Andy's boys are aged two and one. They wander around their
house and garden playing, fighting and spilling things. They definitely

think that they are the bosses! Andy allows them to make lots of very 'significant' decisions: they get to choose between watching *Fireman Sam* and *Thomas the Tank Engine*; they can decide which t-shirt they want to wear; they can pick what toys they want to play with.

However, there is another world that they are completely unaware of. When Judah is about to fall off the table he's climbed on, Andy catches him before he hits the floor. When one wants to sit on the other Andy will distract them with a train or car. When they refuse to eat their vegetables Andy will hide peas inside fish-fingers and shovel them in. Andy's kids think they are in charge – they have no idea! Daddy is at work behind the scenes.

The story of Joseph is the story of a God at work behind the scenes. He does not dictate at every point – he allows people to make mistakes and to face the consequences. This is how children grow up. At the same time, the heavenly Father sees the bigger picture. He guides his children with love and power.

We might wonder: if God was in control, why was Joseph sold as a slave in the first place? Why was he falsely accused of rape? Why did the cupbearer forget him? There are two ways we can ask these questions. The first is as an accusation, to what we believe is a fickle or powerless God. The second is from a place of trust, knowing that there is an answer to those questions, though we can't see what it might be.

No Pit Too Deep

Corrie ten Boom was a modern day 'Joseph'. She and her family lived through World War Two. They ran a watch repair shop in a little Dutch village. When the Nazis occupied Holland and began to hunt down Jews, Corrie and her family, who had been following Jesus for many years, could not stand idly by. Corrie launched a network that smuggled Jews to safehouses around the country. After dodging detection for years the family were eventually betrayed by an informant, and in February of 1944 they were arrested by the Gestapo.

The Hiding Place is Corrie's account of her journey with God through a life that, on the surface, looked to have gone very wrong. When the Gestapo agent saw her elderly father, he offered to have him released if he gave his word not to cause trouble. The old man refused, 'If I go home today,' he said evenly and clearly, 'tomorrow I will open my door again to any man in need who knocks.'[18] He died ten days after being arrested.

Corrie and her sister Betsie were eventually taken to a concentration camp in Germany. Every day was an endurance test. Each new morning brought exposure to the brutal and cruel side of humanity. They were crammed into barracks like animals. They witnessed the madness, depravity and mind-numbing desperation of the thousands they were trapped with. Corrie saw mothers lose their babies within hours of giving birth; she observed the systematic execution of hundreds; the inhumanity of the guards and the loss of her own family.

Yet, just like Joseph, Corrie realised the companionship of God in this place; she discovered that, despite appearances, God was at

18   Corrie ten Boom, *The Hiding Place* (Hodder & Stoughton, 2015) 131.

work. God miraculously provided them with a Bible. They had a little bottle of vitamins that wouldn't run out no matter how much they used it or shared it with others. Day after day they would find, to Corrie's amazement, it had enough vitamins for everyone. Only on the day new bottles of vitamins were finally distributed did the old bottle stop producing.[19]

On one occasion Betsie encouraged Corrie to give thanks in all circumstances. Corrie looked around at the rancid barracks they were crammed into and refused. After some persuasion, she was eventually able to give thanks for the fact that she and Betsie hadn't been separated, and for the people that they had witnessed to. Betsie began to list the things she was thankful for and even included the fleas that infested the place. Corrie drew the line at fleas!

A few weeks later, when Corrie returned from work duties, Betsie was waiting for her triumphantly. She said she had discovered why the guards allowed them so much freedom in their barracks when the other quarters on site were much more closely monitored. It was the fleas. The room was so badly infested the guards refused to enter it! This freedom had allowed the sisters to hold worship services in the heart of a concentration camp. Corrie wrote, 'My mind rushed back to our first hour in this place. I remembered Betsie's bowed head, remembered her thanks to God for creatures I could see no use for.'[20] God even turned fleas into a blessing!

---

19   ten Boom, *The Hiding Place*, 180-189.
20   ten Boom, *The Hiding Place*, 195.

Of course, we might ask why didn't God break Corrie out of jail? As with Joseph, we aren't told. What we do know is that God broke into prison with Corrie. We know her story has gone on to be read by millions, and has pointed them towards the glory and kindness of God. Corrie writes this:

> As the rest of the world grew stranger, one thing became increasingly clear. And that was the reason the two of us were here. Why others should suffer we were not shown. As for us, from morning until lights-out, whenever we were not in ranks for roll call, our Bible was the centre of an ever-widening circle of help and hope. Like waifs clustered around a blazing fire, we gathered about it, holding out our hearts to its warmth and light. The blacker the night around us grew, the brighter and truer and more beautiful burned the word of God ... I would look about us as Betsie read, watching the light leap from face to face ... Life in [the concentration camp] took place on *two separate levels, mutually impossible.* One, the observable, external life, grew every day more horrible. The other, the life we lived with God, grew daily better, truth upon truth, glory upon glory.[21]

Joseph's Discovery

Had Joseph written an autobiography we imagine his words would mirror Corrie's. He experienced life on two levels that seemed mutually incompatible.

---

21   ten Boom, *The Hiding Place*, 182 emphasis ours.

Joseph was a slave, yet we are told he *prospered* as a slave (Gen. 39:2). He was a prisoner and yet he was granted *favour* in prison (v. 21). Sentences like this only make sense when God gets involved.

Life may have gone wrong for you. You might have been through a terrible break up, you may have lost a job or someone you loved, you might have been diagnosed with a terminal illness. Lesson One: God is With Us. We do not write this glibly.

> *Joseph was a slave, yet we are told he prospered as a slave. He was a prisoner and yet he was granted favour in prison. Sentences like this only make sense when God gets involved*

Joseph, and many others, show us that when life throws a punch God is right there. He does not always break us out of the prison, but he never ever abandons us either. He is beside us now. By this we mean his presence is close and his power is sovereign; he is both our companion and the one in control; he is Love and he is Lord. We can know that we will not endure suffering alone, but also that God is able to transform and use our suffering – even as he did Joseph's and Corrie's. Despite all the questions that must have occurred to Joseph along the way, he knew that God could turn pain into blessing, slavery into liberty and prison into prosperity. Or, as Paul wrote, 'that in all things God works for the good of those who love him, who have been called according to his purpose' (Rom. 8:28).

Lesson Two: Turning To God

Bitter or Better?

When life goes wrong we can either turn *from God* and grow bitter, or *to God* and get better. So many of us opt for the first, and our lives end up wrecked on the rock of resentment. Suffering will always change us, but it won't always change us for the better. We have to choose that by turning to God.

> When life goes wrong we can either turn from God and grow bitter, or to God and get better

If there was anyone who could be justified for living in bitterness, it was Joseph. He was just seventeen when he was sold. He was convicted of rape when he was only trying to do the right thing. He spent his 'best years' in prison. Joseph might have easily resented God and the people who had treated him so unjustly. Yet he decided differently.

In Joseph's day vengeance was the way a person dealt with being wronged. Thousands of years later, not much has changed! When our lives go off track there are usually people we *blame* for it. Parents, ex-partners, bosses, friends and even churches can hurt us deeply. We often allow the wounds caused by these hurts to fester. Unforgiveness can be like a cancer. It can spread and kill us spiritually, emotionally and, dare we say it, physically. The Bible

talks of a 'root of bitterness'
(Heb. 12:15). This is when we
allow bitterness to go deep
into our hearts and feed our
whole lives. The only treatment
is forgiveness.

*Unforgiveness can
be like a cancer. It
can spread and kill
us spiritually,
emotionally and,
dare we say it,
physically*

The Medicine of Forgiveness

Of course, to forgive others for
destroying our hopes, dreams,
lives, relationships or self-
worth is easier said than done! Forgiveness sounds like a lovely idea,
until we have someone to forgive. Then it becomes one of the most
difficult things we will ever do!

How did Joseph manage it? What was his secret?

He turned *to God*, not *from God*. He knew God was with him
when he was a slave in Potiphar's house, and that God showed
him favour in the prison. We suspect he didn't focus on the bitterness
he must have felt towards his brothers, or even on getting rid of it.
He focused on God – and in so doing walked out of the bitterness.

ANDY

Some time ago I met a Christian from Northern Nigeria, where
Christians are regularly persecuted. He told me of some of the
friends he had lost.

One friend went to collect a parcel on Christmas Eve. As he and his wife left the post office he needed to tie his shoelace. He put the parcel down, bent down to do his laces, and at that point a bomb exploded. The parcel had been a trap; it was sent to murder the man because of his faith. His wife survived simply because she happened to walk on while he stopped. Another of this man's friends was murdered along with their entire family. They were at home when a gang of extremists attacked them with machetes. They were targeting Christians. The only survivor was a baby a few months old. She will carry a machete scar across her forehead for the rest of her life.

I listened to these and other stories, horrified at what I was being told. Then I asked the question I'd been thinking throughout: 'When these things happen, how do you forgive? How can anyone forgive such brutality?'

The man looked at me for a long time. Then turning away, he told another story. His brother had also been murdered. With no one else to look after her he had since adopted his brother's daughter. He showed me a family photo pointing out his niece standing alongside his other children. Forgiveness, he told me, had been very hard. Indeed, it had taken much internal wrestling to get to that place. The breakthrough moment came when he was kneeling before a little metal cross in a classroom. At this point he finally felt able to release forgiveness toward the murders.

Looking me straight in the eyes again he said, 'How do I forgive, Andy? *By the grace of God.*' I have never forgotten his words.

———————————

By the Grace of God

We in no way want to suggest that forgiveness is an easy or pain-free process. It wasn't for Joseph.

When Joseph's brothers finally turned up in Egypt his reaction was not, 'Hey boys, great to see you, I can finally forgive you in person!' Instead, he embarked on a series of tortuous mind games with them (Gen. 42-45). He accused them of spying, planted evidence in their suitcases and kept Simeon hostage, insisting they return with Benjamin, the youngest brother. When the famine forced their return, Joseph repeated his tricks and this time told the brothers he was keeping Benjamin. The brothers, knowing losing Benjamin would kill their father, begged for mercy. Judah offered himself as a hostage in Benjamin's stead. Only at this point did Joseph crack and reveal his identity.

Why all this game playing?

One possible reason is that Joseph was testing his brothers – he wanted to see that they had come to a place of real repentance. All the evidence suggested that they had. Judah, whose bright idea it had been to sell Joseph in the first place, was now offering to become a slave. Sin has consequences and the brothers had been living with the effects of their sin for over a decade. Joseph was imprisoned in Egypt, but they had been bound by a terrible guilt. They had lived much of their lives with the shadow of their father's grief hanging over them. They were burdened by the appalling secrets they kept and the lies told to cover their tracks. Their moment of impulsive anger had ruined Joseph's life and their father's, and it had destroyed their own lives. The brothers'

Forgiveness is never clinical and neat. We all know it's possible to care for someone and still want to pay them back if they've hurt us

behaviour shows that in their own clumsy way they were trying to make amends.

A second possible reason for Joseph's strange game playing is that *forgiveness is messy*. The moment Joseph saw his brothers, all sorts of powerful and contradictory emotions must have rushed at him. An internal struggle began. He spoke harshly to them, but then withdrew privately to weep. Joseph was a human being, just like us. He loved his brothers and God had worked in him, but it is likely there was still something in him that wanted to punish them. Forgiveness is never clinical and neat. We all know it's possible to care for someone and still want to pay them back if they've hurt us.

Forgiving our Jailers

After the war ended, Corrie ten Boom set up a recovery centre, a place where those seeking restoration and wholeness could come. Corrie also began to travel, sharing her story of God's faithfulness in the midst of severe trial. In *The Hiding Place*, she records the first time she came face to face with one of her former SS guards. This man had mocked and leered at Corrie as she and her sister had been strip searched.

He came up to me as the church was emptying, beaming and bowing. 'How grateful I am for your message *Fraulein*,' he said. 'To think that, as you say, He has washed my sins away!'

His hand was thrust out to shake mine. And I, who had preached so often ... the need to forgive, kept my hand at my side.

Even as the angry, vengeful thoughts boiled through me, I saw the sin of them. Jesus Christ had died for this man; was I going to ask for more? Lord Jesus, I prayed, forgive me and help me to forgive him.

I tried to smile, I struggled to raise my hand. I could not. I felt nothing, not the slightest spark of warmth or charity. And so again I breathed a silent prayer. Jesus, I cannot forgive him. Give me your forgiveness.

As I took his hand the most incredible thing happened. From my shoulder along my arm and through my hand a current seemed to pass from me to him, while into my heart sprang a love for this stranger that almost overwhelmed me.

And so I discovered that it is not on our forgiveness any more than on our goodness that the world's healing hinges, but on His. When He tells us to love our enemies, He gives, along with the command, the love itself.[22]

Forgiveness Brings Freedom

Forgiveness is always a combination of our decision and God's grace. The two need to go together. If we decide we will forgive, that's the moment God steps in to help us. There is of course, a cost to this. However, the price of living in bitterness is always greater.

Forgiveness is always a combination of our decision and God's grace

Peter once asked Jesus how many times he should forgive someone who had sinned against him – he suggested seven as a top-end figure. Jesus answered, 'not seven times, but seventy-seven times' (Matt. 18:22). In other words, we are to forgive as many times as we are sinned against!

In our experience, when we have really been hurt, we have to forgive the *same person*, for *the same thing*, seventy-seven times over! We forgive them, but then – like Joseph and Corrie – we see them again, and the pain or the anger comes back. Whenever we feel resentment, bitterness, hurt or anger try to control us, we have to decide again – we will forgive. At this point it's a *decision* rather

---

22   ten Boom, *The Hiding Place*, 220-1.

than a feeling. Eventually our emotions begin to catch up with this decision.

If Joseph was anything like us, every day in the prison he must have thought, 'My brothers put me here.' Nevertheless he resolved to seek God and release forgiveness. When he finally came face to face with those who had tormented him, grace won the day. Speaking to his terror-stricken brothers Joseph said, 'And now, do not be distressed and do not be angry with yourselves for selling me here, because it was to save lives that God sent me ahead of you' (Gen. 45:5). Joseph was so free from bitterness that he *comforted those who had sold him.*

We cannot control the hand we get dealt in life. We can decide how we respond. It is these decisions, far more than the jail we are in, that determine whether we live in joyous freedom or bitter slavery. Joseph forgave those who had thrown him in jail. When we forgive even those who cause us suffering we discover freedom in the midst of prison. When hurt goes deep there is only one hope we have of being able to forgive: we turn to God, and ask for help.

Lesson Three: When You're Going through Hell, Keep Going

Joseph's story is, eventually, one of dreams wonderfully fulfilled. There must have been many days, however, when he felt as though he was living a nightmare. We get to read with the benefit of hindsight, knowing Joseph became Prince of Egypt, but Joseph didn't know how the story would work out. Living our own story is a different matter entirely from reading someone else's. When it is tough we usually don't know how much longer the struggle will continue. After the storm dies down, perhaps our journey through it becomes a story. In the middle of the storm, however, we are just desperately trying to stay afloat. There is only one way to discover the ending: we have to keep going.

One of our favourite Norwegian proverbs is: 'A hero is someone who hangs on one minute longer.'[23] It encourages both of us when things get tough and we want to quit. After he was thrown into slavery, Joseph might have so easily given up. He could have said, 'I'm done with God, I'm done with "the right thing", and I never want to have another dream.' Instead he demonstrated tremendous staying power. He didn't quit behaving righteously; he refused to sleep with Mrs Potiphar. He didn't stop acting on God's behalf; he interpreted the dreams of the baker and cupbearer. Ultimately, he dug in and stayed faithful, day after day. Thirteen years of slavery and imprisonment meant it was actually 4,745 'day after days'.

4,745 mornings of choosing to live out another day in chains, faithfully.

4,745 evenings of praising God, not knowing whether circumstances would ever change.

4,745 decisions to walk closer to God, not walk away.

4,745 times when the daily resolution to 'dig in' defined the trajectory of Joe's story.

If you are going through hell, keep going!

---

23   That's right, we know enough Norwegian proverbs to have a favourite. (One.)

The Blessing of Suffering

This is a subheading we never thought we'd write!

There is a verse in James' letter that has at times puzzled and fascinated us. He writes, 'Consider it pure joy, my brothers and sisters, whenever you face trials of many kinds, because you know that the testing of your faith produces perseverance. Let perseverance finish its work so that you may be mature and complete, not lacking anything' (1:2-4).

At face value the first statement seems crazy. 'Consider it pure joy when we face trials of many kinds.' What on earth does this mean?

'My cat has been run over – hallelujah!'

'Oh joy, oh happiness … my house has just burnt down!'

God does not cause our suffering, but he works his purposes through it

It doesn't make sense! That is unless you know the God of Scripture. God does not cause our suffering, but he works his purposes through it. Suffering is the only way we develop perseverance. The prize of perseverance is this: that we might be mature and complete, not lacking anything.

The reason most of us are immature, incomplete and lack a lot of things is because we haven't allowed trials of various kinds to develop the gift of perseverance in us. Look at the transformation that took place in Joseph. As a young man of seventeen he was gifted, he heard from God, but he was selfish. Life revolved around him. After thirteen years of hell he was a blessing to others. He didn't lord it over his brothers, he served them and he was used to rescue countless lives from the famine. Thirteen years of clinging to God through trials brought about that transformation.

Keeping Going

If you are going through a difficult time, it can be hard to know *how* to keep going. We all have times when we are desperate to just walk away. Joseph is a great example of perseverance; but Jesus is our ultimate example. The writer to the Hebrews was addressing Christians in the midst of persecution when he wrote, 'Therefore, since we are surrounded by such a great cloud of witnesses, let us throw off everything that hinders and the sin that so easily entangles. And let us run with perseverance the race marked out for us, fixing our eyes on Jesus, the pioneer and perfecter of faith. For the joy set before him he endured the cross, scorning its shame, and sat down at the right hand of the throne of God' (Heb. 12:1-2).

These verses give us clues about to how to keep on keeping on.

Jesus endured the pain and the shame of the cross because there was a joy that was set before him. He could see purpose where others saw meaningless suffering. What was the 'joy' that was set before Jesus? It is astonishing, but *we were*. Jesus already knew perfect intimacy with the Father and the Spirit. The riches of heaven already belonged to him. His goal in coming to earth and enduring the cross was relationship with us. We were the magnificent joy that kept him going!

You may need to pour a cup of tea, stare into space and think about that last sentence for a while.

If we were the joy set before Jesus; he is the joy set before us. The testimony of many saints through the years has been exactly this. They have persevered and triumphed through suffering *because* at the lowest points of their lives they kept sight of the Lord and his presence with them. They saw him who was invisible. They fixed their eyes on Jesus.

ANDY

I once had the privilege of meeting a lady who had escaped from North Korea. North Korea is the worst country in the world when it comes to persecution of Christians. After her conversion this lady had been discovered and sent to a three-year 're-education' camp. She was kept in horrific conditions, forced into manual labour and had to survive on a few spoons of rice a day. As the years went by she was able to share the gospel with her fellow prisoners. Others soon became Christians. They ended up worshipping in the cesspits that were used as toilets – the only place the guards wouldn't follow them. This was their church!

This lady described some of her lowest points: the guards would take her and beat her, seemingly for no reason. She said often at these moments she would have a vision of Jesus, executed on the cross. It was 'seeing' Jesus suffering for her that lent her strength to suffer for him. As I listened to her talk I realised I was meeting someone for whom 'fixing their eyes on Jesus and running the race with perseverance' wasn't a Bible verse, it was a way of life. I resolved to try and do likewise.

There is a risk that saying, 'fix your eyes on Jesus and you'll be able to keep going' sounds clichéd. The truth is, it works; in fact it's the only thing that will. When our goal is our personal happiness we will never attain it. Every time we experience any discomfort we will be plunged into despair and we'll want to quit. When our objective is Jesus, to love, exalt and tell others about him, we will be willing to keeping going through tremendous suffering if it brings us closer to him. It's not that our suffering won't matter to us, it's that our love for Jesus will be more important to us than our comfort. It will be enough to know Jesus is in it, or working through it. One of our favourite hymns captures this:

> *It's not that our suffering won't matter to us, it's that our love for Jesus will be more important to us than our comfort*

O soul are you weary and troubled?
No light in the darkness you see?

> There's light for a look at the Saviour,
> And life more abundant and free:
>
> Turn your eyes upon Jesus,
> Look full in His wonderful face;
> And the things of earth will grow strangely dim
> In the light of His glory and grace.[24]

Many of us can become so overwhelmed by the pain we are experiencing that we lose sight of the Lord of love and power who is sovereignly at work. He will work the evil for good *as we keep going*. It may astonish us what will happen if we take another step and another, one day at a time.

Lesson Four: It's Not About You

Lastly, one of the great lessons Joseph had to learn was that God had called him and blessed him *for the sake of others*. His life was not all about him. At the beginning of Joseph's story we read that he had dreams but there is no hint that he asked God for the interpretation of these dreams; he just announced to his family that they would all bow before him. He would be the big shot!

Oh Joseph! You could have been born in the twenty-first century!

This the selfie generation; we are more obsessed than ever with being at the centre of the photo. This is the celebrity culture where everyone dreams of being famous. There is no doubt that Joseph was anointed, gifted and could hear God when he was a teenager.

---

24   Helen Howarth Lemmel, 'Turn Your Eyes Upon Jesus' (1922), Public Domain.

This, however, is not the basis on which God uses us. In fact what we build in a lifetime with our gifting, we can destroy in a moment with our character. God loved Joseph, so he shaped his character and showed him what the blessing was for.

Blessed to Be A Blessing

Let's look at what happened during Joseph's time in Egypt: 'Joseph found favour in his [Potiphar's] eyes and became his attendant. Potiphar put him in charge of his household, and he entrusted to his care everything he owned. From the time he put him in charge of his household and of all that he owned, the LORD blessed the household of the Egyptian because of Joseph' (Gen. 39:4-5).

The anointing and the gifting were Joseph's – and who got blessed? Potiphar and his household. Joseph was anointed but the slave owner got blessed. This pattern was repeated in prison. Joseph was gifted with interpreting dreams. Who got blessed? The cupbearer. Finally, when Joseph was brought before Pharaoh, he was anointed and gifted, and who was blessed?

Pharaoh – he had a new Prime Minister who made him the richest man in the world.

The Egyptians – their economy prospered and they were able to survive the seven years of famine.

The surrounding nations – they were able to find food because of Joseph's provision.

Finally, Joseph's brothers! The gifting was on Joseph, and amazingly the very family who had sold him into slavery was blessed. As a result of *Joseph's* anointing *they* lived in prosperity till the end of their days.

The Great Reversal

When Joseph revealed himself to his brothers he used a particular phrase, '*God sent me ahead of you*', three times (Gen. 45:5, 7-8). In his culture the people who were sent on ahead were the slaves. They went in advance of their masters to prepare for their master's arrival. Joseph deliberately uses the language of slavery by telling his brothers, 'I was sent ahead of you to Egypt as a slave, to prepare the way for you.' How extraordinary for the man who, at seventeen, thought that the world was going to revolve around him!

We never graduate from being servants. It is not about our fame, but God's glory

Even more amazingly, the language of slavery was also used to describe Jesus: 'Who, being in very nature God, did not consider equality with God something to be used to his own advantage; rather, he made himself nothing by taking the very nature of a servant [slave], being made in human likeness' (Phil. 2:6-7).

God in his mercy will use circumstances to teach us the same lesson. If we are anointed and gifted it is for the sake of others. We never graduate from being servants. It is not about our fame, but God's glory.

In the end Joseph's dreams were fulfilled, but this only happened as he looked to interpret other people's dreams: those of the cupbearer and Pharaoh. When his second son was born Joseph named him Ephraim, saying, 'It is because God has made me fruitful in the land of my suffering' (Gen. 41:52). Joseph didn't deny his pain or suffering, but he declared God had been able to make his suffering fruitful. Joseph was fruitful, but the fruit was for others.

Remarkably, God took the worst thing that happened to Joseph – slavery in Egypt – and turned it into the best thing for Egypt and surrounding nations. Years later God transformed the worst thing that happened to Jesus – the crucifixion – into the great blessing for us and the world around us. It may not feel this way as we sit in the middle of a life gone wrong, but our God is the God of the Great Reversal. He can take our suffering, our pain, our broken life, and bless it – that it might become a blessing to others.

ANDY

Since receiving the news about our baby, Beth and I have had more bad days than good. We feel like a bomb has gone off in our lives; we were heading in one direction; now we're heading in another. I feel so out of control and so helpless. As I write this there is an awful lot that we just don't know. The spectrum between best and worst case scenarios is vast. We have been told that – barring a miracle – the best case scenario is that our son will need heart surgery many times throughout his life; the first when he is a month old.

Over the last few weeks the lessons from the life of Joseph have been going through my mind.

'*God is with us*' – the one who comforts us is also the one in control. The truth that 'God is in charge' has felt like a rubber ring I've been clinging to in the middle of the rapids. I would have drowned without it. I do not understand what is going on and I hate it; but I do believe God understands. He sees the end from the beginning.

'*Turn to God*' – I've been better at this some days than others. Ultimately turning to God has not looked dramatic or impressive. Sometimes it has been quietly crying with God. Other times, sitting with him, not quite able to take in what is happening. Sometimes I have declared his praise and my trust in his character. In times of doubt I have wondered whether he even hears me. Always, however, I have returned to him. I know he is my only hope. The words of Peter come to mind, 'Lord, to whom shall we go? You have the words of eternal life' (John 6:68). Where else can I turn?

'*Keep Going*' – several days into the 'storm' it dawned on me that I wasn't going to be able to make a 'once-for-all' decision to trust God in this situation. I wanted to decide to trust and then be done with it. Like getting a tattoo – once you're inked it's there for life. Sadly, it doesn't work that way. It's much harder. Instead, every day, regardless of how I feel, I have to decide whether I will turn *today* to God's power and love. It is a daily decision of dependence. I don't know how I'll be doing tomorrow, or what it will bring; I just aim to trust God with today.

'*It's not about you*' – God can bless others through you. It remains to be seen how this will work itself out. Already I know

I have a great deal more empathy for those going through something similar. I also know that I have been tremendously blessed by the kindness of others. Beth and I have been inundated by folk who have seen God work through their pain. Some have tales of miraculous healing – stomachs growing, and children that medically 'shouldn't be here'. Others have stories of severe disability and life restricting illness far worse than anything we are facing, but where God is at work. His love and light is fiercely present, burning brightly for all to see. These people and their experiences have blessed me more than I can say. They have given me hope and courage. They have given me confidence that, come what may, we cannot lose. Life goes wrong; God rights wrongs. To go back to the very beginning of this chapter, 'And we know that in all things God works for the good of those who love him, who have been called according to his purpose' (Rom. 8:28).

Read Joseph's Lifeline for Yourself

Joseph's story runs from Genesis 37-50. Some of the key events are:

- Joseph is sold as a slave, Genesis 37:12-36
- Joseph is falsely accused and jailed, Genesis 39
- Joseph interprets Pharaoh's dreams, Genesis 41:1-40
- Joseph is reunited with his brothers, Genesis 42-45

Group Questions

1. Joseph had dreams as a young man. He interpreted them in a very egocentric way. In what ways does our culture (and our sinful humanity) encourage us to make our dreams all about the unholy trinity of 'me, myself and I'?

2. Everything went wrong for Joseph, seemingly in an instant. He went from being the favoured son to a slave in a distant country. Yet it was the making of his character. Can you recognise and recount times when life has seemingly gone wrong and yet you can now see God was at work on you in the mess?

3. Forgiveness is so hard and yet so necessary. What are some of the hardest things you have had to forgive? Talk about the process.

4. We are clearly told that God was with Joseph in his darkest times. Is that your experience? In what ways were you aware that God was with you?

5. The Lord made Joseph fruitful in Egypt, the land of his suffering. What is the land of your suffering? What sort of fruitfulness should you be looking for there?

6. In what ways did Joseph know and experience the blessing of God? Can you name his blessings in your own life?

CHAPTER 5

PREPARING FOR GOD TO USE YOU: LESSONS FROM THE LIFE OF DAVID

David said to Saul, 'Your servant has been keeping his father's sheep.'

1 Samuel 17:34

The Sahara Lounge

What comes to your mind when you imagine heaven?

For one of the authors it is a restaurant in London called The Sahara Lounge. Mike and the head waiter, George, have become good friends. On Mike's recommendation Andy once took his wife there. He mentioned he was Mike's friend. 'Ah Mike!' replied George, enthusiastically, 'He's one of our regulars!' 'How long have you been open for?' Andy asked. 'Just six weeks' replied George. Mike is the only person Andy has met who can be a 'regular' at a six-week old restaurant.

The atmosphere in The Sahara Lounge is warm and inviting. The staff are friendly and hospitable. However, were you to ask

Mike what gives The Sahara Lounge its 5-star status (yes, Mike gives his own star-rating to eateries around the world), he would tell you it is the chicken dish. Mike could spend this entire chapter describing how the chicken melts in the mouth. It has a unique combination of taste and texture that makes it unlike anything else Mike has eaten. He has regularly tried to bribe, manipulate or flatter George into giving him the recipe. (If church leadership one day goes belly-up, his fall-back option is to open a restaurant.) George has remained tight-lipped over the years despite begging, threats and tears. A year ago Mike had a minor breakthrough. George divulged that the chicken was marinated over three days in a top-secret blend of yoghurt, herbs and spices. Then it is cooked slowly over a low heat for many hours.

Surprising though it sounds, George's approach to chicken has something to teach us...

'On the Quick'

There are two mistakes we can make when wanting God to use us. The first: we can think that being chosen or 'anointed' by God is all that is required to be used by him. Once we have our 'God dream' we expect the pieces of our calling to slot swiftly and smoothly into place.

This is partly a result of our culture of instant-everything. We inhabit a world that demands things not so much 'on the cheap' but 'on the quick'. Our stars are social media celebrities; no need to climb the ladder rung by rung – one viral video is all it takes to skip to the top! Those companies able to deliver 'tomorrow' are thriving. Currently 64% of US households have an Amazon Prime membership; in the UK that figure is 33% and climbing. Streaming services guaranteeing instant entertainment are booming. New box sets are now released in a single instalment – no need to wait till next week to find out what happens!

We have grown so accustomed to instant-everything that waiting is infuriating. We can't understand why a song won't download, the traffic jam doesn't move or our big break hasn't arrived. 'Sooner', 'Earlier', 'Faster', 'Straight away', 'Now' are the promises made to us by the advertising we're immersed in. We bring these lenses of instant gratification into our relationship with God.

We have lost count of the number of young people who have shared their dreams with us. They want to be a worship leader, a preacher or a leader in arts, science, education or finance. They often suppose they will have a meteoric, overnight rise to the top, especially because they want to do these things 'for God'. As a result we also often chat to a lot of discouraged people in their twenties and thirties, who are wondering why life hasn't worked out the way they had hoped. We've wanted to cry out to them: 'Train! Practice! Prepare!' It is a good ambition to want to be used by Jesus, but our goal should be surrender, not speed! It is not about anointing or gifting alone.

It is a good ambition to want to be used by Jesus, but our goal should be surrender, not speed! It is not about anointing or gifting alone

God approaches people like George approaches chicken. He prepares them for a long time. We are into microwaving; God is into marinating. He doesn't want us to taste like cardboard; he wants us to have depth of flavour. The Bible has many examples of God's preparation process. Joseph's dreams were followed by thirteen years of God 'marinating' him in prison. Moses had forty years 'marinating' in the desert looking after goats. Even Jesus – who could have begun ministry as soon as he was walking – spent *thirty years* in relative obscurity and just three years in ministry. The first mistake, in an instant world, is we expect our dreams to be fulfilled tomorrow. In so doing, we miss the value of slow preparation.

> *We are into microwaving; God is into marinating*

'Becoming Civilised'

The second mistake we can make is to think that 'preparing to be used by God' no longer applies to us, because we *are* being used by God. We are already doing what he wants us to do!

————————— ANDY —————————

I love the *Rocky* series of films. It started before I was born but contains eternal truths! Rocky Balboa, a down-and-out boxer from a rough part of Philadelphia, gets a shot at the world-heavy-weight title. He takes it and, against the odds, becomes the heavyweight champion of the world. The third Rocky film opens with Rocky living the dream. He has fame, wealth and a raft of endorsements. He has defeated ten title-challengers and is beginning to think about retiring.

Then, at a press conference, a new opponent publicly confronts him – 'Clubber' Lang. Lang goads Rocky into agreeing to fight him. Behind the scenes Mickey – Rocky's trainer – insists the match can't happen. Mickey confesses he has been handpicking easy opponents for Rocky for fear his body is too damaged to survive another beating. Mickey warns him he won't last three rounds with Lang. The reason? Lang is young and powerful but above all he is 'hungry'. Mickey argues that Rocky's pampered life style means he has lost his edge. 'The worst thing that could happen to any fighter has happened to you: you became *civilised*!' Despite this, Rocky persuades Mickey to let him fight – he vows to 'live in the gym'.

Forgetting his promise, however, Rocky's training is full of press conferences, distractions and parties. Lang, on the other hand, trains with ruthless determination. The match sees Lang dominate an ill-equipped Rocky. He is overwhelmed by the ferocity of what hits him and defeated in a second round knock-out. The rest of the film portrays the soul searching journey Rocky goes on as a result of this humiliation. He returns to his roots and rediscovers the hunger that he once had – *the Eye of the Tiger*. This rekindled desire drives him to train harder, longer and with greater passion than ever before. (It also involves some epic 80s training montages you can now watch on YouTube.) The film ends with Rocky – in the best fighting shape of his career – triumphing over Lang.

Rocky's story is a parable for us. Time, age, experience and even success can blunt our hunger for God to use us. After years following Jesus, without realising it, we can switch into cruise control and begin to coast. From the outside we may still look like we are following Jesus. We talk a good game, and score a few quick wins now and then – we are doing what we think we've been told to do. But inside, the radical, passionate, give-it-all fire has flickered and faded. Risks we would have once taken we now shy away from. Aspirations we used to have we've put to one side. Sacrifices we might have once made we are now too 'grown-up' to consider. Our once focused desire to 'seek the kingdom' has become distorted and blurred. The worst thing that could happen to any follower of the mighty, uncontainable Jesus Christ has happened to us: we have softened, settled and grown comfortable. We too, have become civilised.

Jesus promised that everyone who bears fruit would be ... pruned!

In our early years following Jesus, he will instil in us lessons he never wants us to forget. However, God is always training us! Throughout our lives he will repeatedly take us through seasons of being stripped back. In John 15:2 Jesus promised that everyone who bears fruit would be ... high-fived? Rewarded? Promoted? No – *pruned*! In other words, put through more 'training' that they might be even more fruitful. During these seasons God is getting us ready to be used by him.

Catching God's Eye

When we talk of God 'preparing us' and wanting us to have a 'depth of flavour,' what exactly do we mean? What is God searching for in those he uses?

David's story gives us the answer.

It begins with God sending the prophet Samuel to Bethlehem. God was hunting for a new king and had seen someone for the job – the son of a man named Jesse. Samuel arrived; Jesse gathered his boys and brought them one by one before the prophet.

'Samuel saw Eliab and thought, "Surely the LORD's anointed stands here before the LORD." But the LORD said to Samuel, "Do not consider his appearance or his height, for I have rejected him. The LORD does not look at the things people look at. People look at the outward appearance, but the LORD looks at the heart"' (1 Sam. 16:7).

Samuel told Jesse, 'It's not Eliab.' And so Abinadab, the second son came forward. 'The LORD has not chosen this one either,' said Samuel. Seven of Jesse's sons were brought to Samuel, but Samuel said, 'The LORD has not chosen these.' Finally, in confusion, Samuel asked Jesse, '"Are these all the sons you have?" "There is still the youngest," Jesse answered. "He is tending the sheep." Samuel said, "Send for him; we will not sit down until he arrives"' (1 Sam. 16:11).

Eventually David was brought in. Samuel saw God's hand on his life and in the presence of his older brothers anointed him as the new king! This is a little like the Prime Minister turning up at our home demanding to see the children of the household. All seven of our older siblings are brought in and turned down; finally, we are texted and told to come home from walking the dogs. The moment she lays eyes on us the Prime Minister exclaims, 'You are the one our country needs!' and in front of our entire family places a crown upon our head. This happened to David! What a moment to savour!

Why did God choose David, a young boy, and not the seven other sons of Jesse? Or for that matter, why David and not all the other people living in Israel? The answer is found in God's words to Samuel: 'The LORD does not look at the things people look at. People look at the outward appearance, but the LORD looks at the heart.'

Appearance matters in our world. It is the way we judge. Sadly this is just as often the case in the church. 'Is a person clever, gifted, funny or handsome enough for God to use them?' we wonder. 'Am I?' 'Do I have the personality, the skillset or the charisma?' We compare ourselves to each other. In doing this, we reveal that *we don't yet understand what catches God's eye.* Our salaries or exam grades do not impress him, nor do our business deals or sports skills, our cars or our clothes. Someone might captivate the whole world but be rejected for a position of prominence in God's kingdom. Equally those often overlooked by our world can grab God's attention. In David's case, he was forgotten about – he wasn't even invited to the party with Samuel! But God had seen something he couldn't take his eyes off: a heart turned towards him.

A Heart After God

David is described as 'a man after God's own heart' (1 Sam. 13:14). It is our hearts, not our CV that God is interested in. What is God considering when he looks at someone's heart?

Humility

First, God is looking for humility. The statement, 'God opposes the proud and shows favour to the humble' is found three times in the Bible (Prov. 3:34, James 4:6 and 1 Pet. 5:5). God seems to *love* humility. Humility is not low self-esteem. As Rick Warren helpfully defines it, 'Humility is not thinking less of yourself, it's thinking of yourself less.' Humble people are teachable; they are open to learning and growing. A humble heart will mean we don't 'settle' or become complacent in our walk with God. Pride says, 'There's nothing more to learn; I've arrived.' Humility says, 'Every day is a "school day"; I can always grow; I can always improve.' Pride leads us to put ourselves first; humility causes us to prefer others. Humility means we are open to correction; we understand we will get things wrong, hurt others or let God down. Humble people are quick to say sorry. Having a heart after God does not mean never sinning, it means we are quick to return to him when we do.

David's humble heart was evident throughout his life but perhaps most memorably when the prophet Nathan confronted him (2 Sam. 12). David, ruler of all Israel by this stage, had had an affair with Bathsheba and murdered her husband to cover up the sin. Nathan, sent by God, denounced him publicly in the throne room. Any other king might well have had Nathan's

Having a heart after God does not mean never sinning, it means we are quick to return to him when we do

head at that point! Supreme rulers generally do what they want and very few powerful people are able to receive public correction. David's sin was terrible, but his reaction to being called on it tells us everything. He is distraught and grief-ridden. He cries out to God for mercy; he repents. From this place he famously wrote Psalm 51. It is the psalm of 'sorry': 'My sacrifice, O God, is a broken spirit; a broken and contrite heart you, God, will not despise' (Ps. 51:17).

Devotion

God sees all things, but he *searches* for some things. Secondly, he is looking for hearts devoted to him – hearts that place him before all else. In 2 Chronicles 16:9 we read, 'For the eyes of the LORD range throughout the earth to strengthen those whose hearts are fully committed to him.'

David's psalms display a heart that overflowed with praise and adoration of God: 'One thing I ask from the LORD, this only do I seek: that I may dwell in the house of the LORD all the days of my life, to gaze on the beauty of the LORD and to seek him in his temple' (Ps. 27:4). The *one thing* David sought wasn't money, armies or George's chicken recipe. It was God himself. God delights in using people who care more for *him* than for any position or role they are given.

On one occasion David brought the Ark of the Covenant to Jerusalem. He organised a huge festival celebrating God and his goodness. Thousands thronged the streets of the city. Right there, in the middle of the crowd, David worshipped God. He leapt and danced with abandonment wearing nothing but a linen ephod (something the size of a tea towel!). Imagine watching the Queen attending church and dancing around in her swimwear! His wife, Michal, was not impressed. In her eyes her husband had embarrassed himself and when he got home she gave him a piece of her mind! David's response is revealing; he couldn't believe she had missed the point. He hadn't even *noticed* the crowds when he had worshipped; he was living for an Audience of One: 'It was before the LORD, who chose me ... when he appointed me ruler over the LORD's people Israel – I will celebrate before the LORD. I will become even more undignified than this, and I will be humiliated in my own eyes' (2 Sam. 6:21-22). This is an astonishing statement – how many of us could honestly say we would become undignified, foolish, demeaned or dishonoured if it glorified God? No wonder David's heart had God's attention.

Dependency

Third, God is looking for hearts that depend on him. So many of us try to 'go it alone'. We think God wants us to be independent and that 'maturity' is being able to do the tasks we've been given without needing help. The truth is entirely the opposite. The most mature and established believers are the most dependent ones. God works best with his friends, those who know they need him to accomplish anything of eternal worth and who stick close.

David was a very flawed human being. He sinned, failed and made mistakes. He wept, grew discouraged and at times was full of fear. His great secret was not that he was more capable than anyone

*His great secret
was not that he
was more capable
than anyone else;
it was that for all
his brokenness he
leaned on God*

else; it was that for all his bro-kenness he leaned on God. Even after David became powerful he looked to his God for help.

Psalm after psalm records David's vulnerable, confused, poignant cries to God. 'Save me, O God, for the waters have come up to my neck. I sink in the miry depths, where there is no foothold ... I am worn out calling for help; my throat is parched. My eyes fail, looking for my God' (69:1-3). These songs give us a glimpse of the attitude of raw, trusting dependency that characterised David's relationship with his God.

The Heavenly Gym

Perhaps you are reading this thinking – 'Uh oh! I struggle to be humble, devoted and dependent. God can clearly never use me!' Welcome to our club! We feel the same way (apart from humility – we've cracked that one).

The good news is that there is something we *can* do. David wasn't simply anointed by God; he was *prepared* by him. We might have expected David to head straight to the palace after Samuel had anointed him and measure up for new curtains. Instead he did something remarkable: he went back to looking after the sheep.

There are three things to know about shepherding in David's day:

- It was boring (not even Netflix to pass the time).
- It was hidden (no 'Shepherd of the Year' competition to enter).
- It was lonely (no WhatsApp to share sheep stories).

In this boring, hidden and lonely place David's heart continued to be nurtured and his skills honed. Strange as it might seem, he learnt how to be the shepherd of Israel by shepherding sheep. In our world of fast-paced entertainment, instant 'likes' and constant connection we shy away from anything that is boring, hidden or lonely. This place, however, is the heavenly gym; it is a training ground. We may not have a heart that is especially humble, devoted or dependent, *but we do have a choice we can make.* We can choose to embrace the role God has for us in the boring, hidden and lonely place. If we do so, not only will God prepare our hearts to be used by him, he will also teach us the practical skills we'll need for the tasks ahead.

Learning to Fight

–––––––––––––––––––––––––– MIKE ––––––––––––––––––––––––––

Andy might like boxing films but I prefer martial arts. One of my favourites is *The Karate Kid*. It is the story of a teenager, Daniel, who goes to a new school and is bullied by a group who are into karate. Daniel meets an elderly Japanese man, Mr Miyagi, who happens to be a Karate master. Daniel convinces him to take him on as a student. The training, however, is not what he expects. Mr Miyagi sets Daniel a lot of long, menial chores. He has to sand the deck, wax the car, and paint Mr Miyagi's fence and house. In great frustration Daniel finally confronts his teacher and announces he is quitting. He cannot see how painting fences has anything to do with Karate!

At this point Mr Miyagi demands Daniel repeat the circular motion he used to sand the deck. Daniel waves his hands through the air. Mr Miyagi then orders him to perform the movement he used to wax the car – wax on, wax off. He tells him to make the side-to-side brushstroke he used to paint the house and the up-and-down motion for painting the fence. Then Mr Miyagi attacks Daniel! Before Daniel realises what is happening his reflexes have kicked in. He uses the circular, up-down, side-to-side movements automatically to block Mr Miyagi's attack. They stand there in silence. In shock, it dawns on Daniel: he thought he was just waxing a car, or painting a house, but in truth he was learning the very skills he needed for Karate.

Bears to Giants

David burst onto the public scene in 1 Samuel 17. The three-metre Philistine giant, Goliath, was terrifying the Israelite army. Day after day he would challenge any of them to fight him. None of the soldiers were up to the job. Fortunately, at that point a shepherd arrived …

Visiting the frontline to bring food for his brothers, David overheard Goliath's challenge. Curious, he asked the soldiers about it: 'When Eliab, David's oldest brother, heard him speaking with the men, he burned with anger at him and asked, "Why have you come down here? And with whom did you leave those few sheep in the wilderness? I know how conceited you are and how wicked your heart is; you came down only to watch the battle"' (v. 17:28).

Eliab, no doubt with the image of Samuel anointing David at the back of his mind, humiliated his little brother. He insulted the very thing that God had commended David for – his heart! It's as if to say, 'God might see this in you, but *I* know the truth!' How many of us have had God commend us for something only to have someone mock that very affirmation?

At this point, David's whole destiny might have changed. He could so easily have taken offence and gone home. We often meet people living in the twilight zone of church who have done just that. They refuse to really commit because someone hurt them years ago. Alternatively, David could have believed what Eliab thought about his prospects, rather than trusting what God had spoken to him. Many of us listen more to the voices of the people around us than to our Father. We can miss our calling because of others' accusations or attitudes. We cannot control what others say to us but we do have power over our response. David simply shrugged his shoulders, and went on asking his questions.

Eventually word reached King Saul and David was brought before him. 'I'll fight the giant,' said the courageous kid to the terrified king. Saul pointed out what everyone else was thinking: 'You are not able to go out against this Philistine and fight him; you are only a young man, and he has been a warrior from his youth' (v. 33). David then gave Saul a list of his qualifications. They did not include time in the army. Instead, he stated: *'Your servant has been keeping his father's sheep.'*

Whilst neither of us have ever applied to join the Royal Marines, we are pretty sure that 'looking after sheep' would not be the first thing on our resumé if we did! However, David went on to explain himself: 'When a lion or a bear came and carried off a sheep from the flock, I went after it, struck it and rescued the sheep from its mouth. When it turned on me, I seized it by its hair, struck it and killed it. Your servant has killed both the lion and the bear; this uncircumcised Philistine will be like one of them ... The LORD who rescued me from the paw of the lion and the paw of the bear will rescue me from the hand of this Philistine' (vv. 34-37).

David spent night and day in the wilderness protecting sheep from wild animals. Approaching the battle line he saw just another bear – Goliath – attacking some frightened sheep – the Israelite army. Saul offered David his weapons to fight with, the best money could buy, and David refused. He opted for what he was used to; the weapons he had been using day in day out, to protect the sheep his dad, Jesse, had assigned to him. Now it was time to use those same skills to protect the people his heavenly Father was entrusting to him.

We are to embrace whatever tasks God has put before us. If David had avoided defending the sheep, he would never have defended Israel. Our current role may seem boring and dull, but in giving ourselves to it we will be developing skills that will serve us in the future. That might sound as ludicrous as painting fences seemed to Daniel, but God is an expert trainer, and he knows what he is doing. He sees the end from the beginning and understands what our tomorrow will hold. This means that as impossible and unlikely as it might seem to us in our present school, workplace or home situation, God is able to teach us what we need to know. He is preparing us for tomorrow's giant.

If David had avoided defending the sheep, he would never have defended Israel

Learning to Worship

Many of us are not in the place we want to be. We feel that life, like a video buffering, has got stuck. No matter how many times we press 'refresh' we cannot move it on. Our job is to do our homework or turn up to band practice; it's to do the accounts, stack the shelves or change another nappy. It feels like others are being recognised, admired and appreciated, all whilst we are stuck in a rut. We certainly don't feel like we are on God's radar.

We might be surprised to discover we are being marinated. This is a time for our flavour to develop; for our character to deepen.

This is *exactly the place* where we grow. It does, however, involve a decision to see this season as training time. What exactly is God wanting to teach us?

The Secret Chord

Fighting was not all that David learned during his years as a shepherd. Israel's fiercest warrior also became her greatest worshipper. Many of the psalms are attributed to David; they have since been sung down the centuries by billions of people. When evil spirits tormented Saul, David would play and the spirits would flee. Before David's songs gave a voice to the souls of billions, the sheep, the stars and his God heard them.

> *Before David's songs gave a voice to the souls of billions, the sheep, the stars and his God heard them*

We strongly suspect that his most famous song, 'The LORD is my shepherd, I lack nothing' (Ps. 23:1), was not composed in a palace but on the lonely side of a hill, at three o'clock in the morning. We imagine those chords were first played for God's ears alone. The secret place, the place no one is watching, applauding or appreciating, is *the place* we learn to sing to our Father. This includes sung worship; it also includes lives of worship.

Our friend Matt Redman has now written many songs that are being sung all over the world. He is particularly known for the depth of his lyrics, which are rooted in Scripture. He leads worship skilfully in many nations. Mike has known Matt since he was thirteen years old and knows that Matt didn't wake up one morning with these gifts fully formed. Matt knew he was called to be a worship leader and he prepared. It involved sacrifice. Matt gave up some of his other passions, things he enjoyed, because he felt that God had told him to put them to one side. Mike and Matt decided to meet to worship Jesus regularly. At Matt's suggestion they opted for 'the best night of the week', Saturday evening. Day after day when Matt could have been at parties or the cinema he spent time in his room practising his guitar, playing and worshipping Jesus on his own. The last thing he would do at night before going to sleep would be to read Scripture. We could describe that time as 'boring, lonely and hidden' or we could see it as essential preparation – preparation that Matt embraced whole-heartedly.

Most of us will not be called to be worship leaders; we are all called to be worshippers. If we are to really dance for an Audience of One, there's no better place to practise than when it feels like no one is appreciating us. This is where we get to train ourselves to do the things only God will see. The Baptist preacher Charles Spurgeon once asked a domestic servant girl what difference her becoming a Christian had made. She replied, 'Now I sweep under the mats.' She cleaned the parts of the house that no one ever checked. We can sing to God in the car, in the shower and in our rooms – sing and dance when only he sees. We can also change the nappies, complete the assignment, and even do an extra lap on the track for him. Let it be worship. This isn't something that happens accidentally; we have to embrace our current season because we know that it is God's place for us. A heart to worship is not formed in the spotlight, but in the shadows.

Learning to Lead

We suspect David also learned a lot about leading people by shepherding sheep.

Sheep don't do what they are told; they panic easily and wander off aimlessly, just like us! David had to have patience with Israel and he got to practise this day after day in the hills of Judea. Sometimes leadership is a difficult job; people do not always appreciate the sacrifices made for them. David must have become an expert in laying down his life for those who didn't thank him. He would risk being mauled to death by a bear and the sheep would amble away, not even stopping to 'baa' politely. Yet all the evidence is that David devoted himself to his few sheep, caring for them deeply. This is what made him so ready to care for a numerous people.

Jesus once told a parable about a master who gave his servants bags of gold (Matt. 25:14-30). The master went away and on his return demanded to know what had been done with the gold – had it been invested well? To those servants who had put the money to work and multiplied it, he gave more. To the servant who had not, he took away even what he had. What are we doing to invest what God has *already* given to us?

Many of us entertain the idea that we will be generous with our money when we have more of it. If we are not generous now, surprising as it sounds, winning the lottery will not create true generosity in us. Some of us think, 'When I get to a position where I am satisfied and significant, *then* I will encourage and raise up other people.' The truth is that

What are we doing to invest what God has already given to us?

if we are not encouraging others now, a promotion will not transform us.

Some of us think, 'When my circumstances have sorted themselves out, then I will worship God.' We miss that if we don't worship God in the darkness, our worship will be short-lived in the light. We can sit around wishing for a shot at the 'big time' and miss what is right in front of us. The best way to be given more responsibility by God is to take responsibility for what we have been given. We will not care for the church if we don't care for our youth group; we will not love the staff when we are the manager if we don't love them when we're not. Love, give, serve and encourage in the seemingly 'small things' of now.

Your Hidden Place

Let us ask you some questions:

Where are your Judean hills? Where are you investing in 'a few sheep'?

Are you impatient for a platform of some kind, or are you embracing preparation in the hidden place?

We know too many who have missed walking into their calling because they didn't grasp the seasons when God was training them. They didn't stay in the boring, hidden and lonely place where their hearts could be nurtured and their gifts honed. When they finally came face to face with their giants they didn't know how to fight. Let us leave you with two of Mike's heroes.

--------------------------------- MIKE ---------------------------------

One of my heroes is the late James Ryle. He was one of the best Bible teachers I have ever heard – and I've heard a lot! James taught from the Scripture with eloquence, passion and depth of insight. This is his story: Before he became a Christian he was driving a car whilst high on drugs. He lost control of the car and one of his passengers died. James was convicted of homicide and jailed. At the time of his trial he met Jesus and became a Christian. He sensed from the beginning a call from God to preach the gospel. He still had to face years in prison. Prison has to be one of the most lonely, boring and hidden places there is but James believed that God had a destiny for his life. So in that prison he prepared. He read the dictionary from A-Z, memorising the words and their meanings. He prepared and sculpted his vocabulary and ability to communicate. He shared the good news of Jesus with anyone who would hear him – prisoner or guard. He read some of the classic pieces of literature in the English language, to enrich his mind. Years later, when he came out of prison, he was ready. God used James very powerfully in his final years.

Another of my heroes is not a spiritual giant, but a footballing one. As a Manchester United fan, I consider David Beckham one of 'the greats of our time'. He is up there with presidents, Nobel laureates and my friend George. I remember watching an interview with him about how he became a sensational footballer. He talked about the way he spent his teenage years: 'After school I would go to the back of my house and kick the ball against the wall. I kicked it for hours. I kicked it with my right foot. Then I kicked it with my left foot. I kicked it again and again. That's all I did.' No doubt Beckham had talent and ability, but what made the difference were the hours he spent on his own at the back of his house kicking the ball against the wall. It would have been lonely when all his friends were hanging out. It had to have been boring. It was hidden. But it was by facing that wall at the back of the house that Beckham became the legendary footballer he was.

God has fruit he wants all of us to bear. It may be through preaching and it may be through football. One thing is certain: because he loves us and wants us to be the best we can be, he also wants to prepare us. Don't shun this; *welcome* it. If you are in a season of the boring, hidden and lonely, even (and especially) if it feels like a long season, *embrace it.* Serve, worship and practise when no one but God sees. Here we develop depth. What is more, stay hungry; *seek* this training out. God will never stop preparing us for the next step; there is always more. God promised David: 'I will make your name great, like the names of the greatest men on earth' (2 Sam. 7:9). He used sheep to accomplish this. He is using our version of sheep to shape us. Wow, he must have some big plans ahead!

Read David's Lifeline for Yourself:

- 1 Sam. 16 – 1 Kings 2
- 1 Chron. 11-29

Chronicles retells some of the story of David, but from a different perspective. His worst moments — especially the sin with Bathsheba — are not recorded.

Group Questions

1. Instant spirituality is usually shallow spirituality. Discuss.
2. In what areas of your life do you recognise the influence of our quick fix culture?
3. Describe one of your boring, lonely and hidden places. In what ways can you see God at work on your character in those times?
4. How can we encourage each other to let God 'cook us slowly' so that we taste delicious to a broken and hurting world?
5. In your experience what is the worst aspect of the boring, lonely and hidden place?
6. Which truths of Scripture could you meditate on in the hidden times?

CHAPTER 6

THRIVING IN AN ALIEN CULTURE: LESSONS FROM THE LIFE OF DANIEL

My prayer is not that you take them out of the world but that you protect them from the evil one. They are not of the world, even as I am not of it.

John 17:15-16

A Visitor to University

One of the authors attained a first class degree in theology from Cambridge University. (The other author would like you to know that he passed his driving test – second time.)

ANDY

When I was a student, Richard Dawkins visited Cambridge to promote his recently published book *The God Delusion*. The book had been hitting the headlines and so I went along to hear what he had to say. The two-tiered, wooden-panelled debating chamber was packed to the rafters with students like myself, all keen for a glimpse of the famous atheist. During the evening Dawkins read book extracts to his attentive audience.

I vividly remember him reading the following: 'The God of the Old Testament is arguably the most unpleasant character in all fiction: jealous and proud of it; a petty, unjust, unforgiving control freak; a vindictive, bloodthirsty ethnic cleanser; a misogynistic, homophobic, racist, infanticidal, genocidal, filicidal, pestilential, megalomaniacal, sadomasochistic, capriciously malevolent bully.'[25]

As he finished I was shocked to hear the room fill with cheers and applause. People weren't just enjoying his prose; they clearly thought he was right! I was used to hostility towards Christianity. What troubled me this time, however, was the angry, careless and disparaging way belief in God was being mocked. It seemed that Dawkins had at best skim-read a few sections of the Bible and reached some highly questionable conclusions. Yet here he was being wildly cheered. Afterwards I wandered to a party nearby. There I met a girl who had also attended Dawkins' event. I started to share my unease at the reaction students had given to Dawkins – then I caught the look on her face and realised she must have been one of them. I then listened to her tell me about the dangers of religion and its lack of any real basis in fact.

------

25   Richard Dawkins, *The God Delusion* (Black Swan, 2007) 51.

Living in a Hostile World

Although Dawkins is a somewhat extreme and militant example, these attitudes pervade much of our culture. In whole sections of our universities and media Christianity is regarded as at best a naïve, unscientific set of beliefs, and at worst positively dangerous to a society that is marching away from 'myths' and 'fairy tales'. The occasional royal wedding in a church and the many spires we drive past can lull us into thinking that ours is a Christian culture. Perhaps this was once the case; it certainly is not now. Even when we don't encounter open aggression towards Christianity there is a clash of worlds taking place around us.

The foundational message of our culture is 'Be who *you* want to be; do what *you* want to do! Don't let anyone else stop you. Express yourself!' In other words, our individual freedom is the supreme good. This is very different from the message of Jesus, and the basis of the kingdom of heaven. The message Jesus preached was not, 'Express yourself for your sake'; it was, 'Deny yourself for my sake.' He told us to take up our cross and to follow him! Human rights mattered to Jesus, but he willingly surrendered his own. He showed us that there was something greater than

> *The message Jesus preached was not, 'Express yourself for your sake'; it was, 'Deny yourself for my sake'*

individual freedom – sacrificial love. To be Jesus' follower is to believe in laying down our rights and freedoms for Jesus' sake. As we do this we are transformed.

Christians make decisions based on a very different approach to life from those around us. What this means, of course is on some issues we will think and act the same as our non-Christian friends, family or colleagues. But it also means there will be plenty of moments when we seem strange, or even crazy, to those not yet following Jesus. They may not understand why we are making certain choices involving our time, money or lifestyle. We will find ourselves sticking out, at odds with those around us, being different. It can be hard to know what to do when this happens.

We usually make one of two mistakes: first, in an effort to be 'relevant', we immerse ourselves in the culture around us. Soon we look, talk, act and think so like our world that there is nothing that sets us apart. Second, in an attempt to be 'holy', we run away from the culture into our Christian ghetto. Separate and cut off, we end up unable to communicate God's counter-cultural truth in a loving way to the world around us. The light is meant to shine in the darkness, not be hidden away safely in a room full of other lights.

This is a journey all of us must negotiate!

How can we be *in* the school but not *of* the school? *In* the workplace but not *of* the workplace? *In* the family but not *of* the family? *In* the world, but not *of* the world? How do we walk Jesus' path when the surrounding culture wants us to walk its own?

Welcome to Babylon

There is a character in the Bible who faced all of the issues of living in a culture alien to his beliefs. Wonderfully, he didn't just survive, he thrived. His name was Daniel, and, as with so many of our lifelines, his story is worthy of being made into a multi-million pound blockbuster.

All great stories have a villain. Daniel's was Nebuchadnezzar – the ruler of the Babylonian empire. He was a nasty piece of work! Nebuchadnezzar would capture rulers who defied him along with their entire families. He would force the ruler to watch as he executed his children, before ripping out the ruler's eyes. The blinded, chained, broken ruler would then be brought to live out the rest of his days in Babylon. And we thought Sauron from *The Lord of the Rings* was cruel!

Unfortunately for Daniel, Nebuchadnezzar had expansion in mind and Jerusalem in his sights. He captured and laid waste to the city and tore many of the elite young men away from their families. They were brought as prisoners to Babylon. King Neb was cunning. He knew he couldn't rule a huge empire full of diverse people groups by military force alone and so he had a plan. He aimed to infuse impressionable young men with the Babylonian DNA after which he would send them back to their homelands as his representatives. The goal was to brainwash them. Among these captives were Daniel and his three friends.

The moment the boys arrived, the brainwashing began. The first things to go were their Hebrew names. Each name testified to God. The friends were renamed after the Babylonian gods, and so

Hananiah, Mishael, and Azariah became Shadrach, Meshach and Abednego. Daniel, whose name meant 'God is my Judge', was renamed Belteshazzar, meaning 'May Bel protect his life'. Bel was the chief of Babylon's many gods. The second things to go – and it pains us to even write this – were probably the friends' testicles. We're not told this explicitly but it's probable the four young men were castrated.[26]

Lastly King Neb had the friends educated in the language and literature of the Babylonians. For three years they were to be immersed in Babylon's values and belief system. In the case of Daniel, Hananiah, Azariah and Mishael, Neb's objective was simple: when they had finished the programme of cultural indoctrination, on the *outside* they might still look Jewish – but *inside* they would be Babylonian.

How Can We Relate to This?

Question (ladies, leave out one key aspect):
Imagine you were kidnapped and taken to the other side of the world to a place with completely different customs and spiritual practices. You were enslaved, you had your name changed to honour their gods and

---

26   We know that in Babylon many slaves were castrated. There's no evidence that Daniel and his friends ever married. In Isaiah 39:5-7 there's a prophecy that young men would be taken to Babylon and become eunuchs in the palace of the king of Babylon. The Hebrew word *saris* is used to describe the man in charge of Daniel (1:3); this can mean a 'government official' in general, but it is also the specific word used to describe a man castrated in order to fulfil a political or religious role. It is likely he was 'chief of the eunuchs.'

your testicles were removed. Imagine you spent the next three years being indoctrinated in the language, literature and culture of this foreign country. How do you think your faith would be doing?

This story is so far removed from us it can be hard to see any connection. However, today something similar *is* happening. Satan is attacking the church and he is using our culture to do so. His goal is to take Christians and so indoctrinate us in the culture around us that we end up castrated: spiritual eunuchs. 'Christians' in name but not practice. Jesus followers on the outside but society followers on the inside.

How many of us are willing to go against the flow of those around us when it comes to love, sacrifice and living for the sake of others?

This is where Daniel and friends can help us – there are vital lessons we can learn as we inhabit our modern Babylon. It begins with recognising that Babylon had a two-pronged attack: seduction and intimidation.[27]

Attack One: Seduction

Tuck In

Arriving in Babylon must have been quite something for Daniel. He had lived in Jerusalem, at that time an impoverished city. In contrast, Babylon was the grandest city on earth. Its architecture, temples and idols would have been on a scale the boys had never

---

27   J Philip and S Cherian, *Four Men Against A Kingdom,* Kindle Edition Chapter 1 paragraph 2 (Philip Communications, 2015).

seen. The hanging gardens of Babylon, built by Nebuchadnezzar, were one of the seven wonders of the ancient world. The last view the boys had of their home was a smoking pile of ruins; they were now marched into the heart of enemy power – an enormous metropolis, oozing wealth and strength.

The new living arrangements were explained and remarkably the friends found 'The king assigned them a daily amount of food and wine from the king's table' (Dan. 1:5). Understand that this is not just any old food. *Marks and Spencer* once released an advert. As it begins, sultry music is played; items of delicious-looking cuisine are speared in slow motion, while a woman huskily whispers: 'Traditionally cured Scottish gravlax salmon with creamy mustard and dill sauce. Hand-prepared turkey with Braeburn apple and sage stuffing, wrapped in maple cured bacon. Lincolnshire red cabbage, with apple and cranberries, slow-braised in red-wine and tawny port sauce. Golden roast parsnips, coated with wildflower honey and mustard dressing ....'

[Author's Note: For the remainder of this chapter Andy will be writing solo. Mike has just popped to *Marks and Spencer*.]

The strapline: '*This isn't just food, this is M&S food*', could be applied here: '*This isn't just food, this is the king's table food.*' The boys have arrived! The best of Babylon is within their reach. The hummus and pitta they've been raised on is a thing of the past! Imagine getting taken into 'exile' only to find you were going to be *made* to eat in a five-star restaurant for the rest of your life!

We don't think we would have a problem with that. Daniel, on the other hand did: 'But Daniel resolved not to defile himself with the royal food and wine' (v. 8). At first glance this is a bit of a puzzle. The boys didn't object to their names being changed and they didn't say no to studying the literature of the Babylonians. In the years to come Daniel didn't even turn down the post as head of the department of magicians, sorcerers and diviners (5:11)! Yet he drew the line at a sausage roll.

Why?

Who is Your Boss?

Daniel's refusal to eat the food might seem like a small thing; it was, however, a huge decision. We understand this when we appreciate that it was not a test of Daniel's dieting skills; *it was a test of his loyalty.*

The Jewish law set out clear commands about what food God's people were not allowed to eat. Certain foods were 'clean' and others 'unclean'. Some of the food from the king's table would definitely have fallen into the 'unclean' category. Moreover, the law didn't allow the Jews to eat meat that still had blood in it – something unlikely to be considered by the king's kitchens (Lev. 11; 17:10-12). Whilst the law said nothing about wine, it's likely that at least some of the wine (and food) at the king's table had been offered to Babylonian gods. (This happened at the feast in Daniel 5:4.) This is exactly the sort of wine Daniel didn't want to be filled with!

This was not about appetite; it was about allegiance. Would Daniel eat what he was given and in doing so acknowledge Neb as his master? That would have seemed prudent, surrounded as he was by a display of the might and power of King Neb. Daniel, however, knew his true master was the King of Kings; it was to him his allegiance was sworn. Knowing this, his decision was not complicated; the Scripture spoke plainly enough. The food was a no-go.

Some of the challenges we'll experience in our culture will be the same. God will tell us one thing in his Word; the culture will suggest something contradictory. There are times when our difficulty is to correctly understand and apply what the Bible says to today's context. There are many more times, however, when the Biblical direction is plain and clear. These are moments when our loyalty is tested. Who is the boss? To whom does our allegiance belong?

As a young man, Daniel grasped that the seemingly small decisions had big implications. If he was unable to be obedient when it came to his knife and fork he had no chance when the bigger challenges came. He nailed his colours to the mast; he was following God – regardless of what everyone else was eating.

Who Are We Depending On?

Make no mistake, there is a bigger picture here than simply obedience, the law and loyalty. Daniel's resolve not to eat the king's food was also a way of guarding his heart. Hidden within the offer of the best food in the empire was Babylon's attempt to win not just its captives' stomachs but their souls as well. King Neb was using the best Babylon could offer to seduce the exiles. He set himself up as the 'provider' and the captives as the 'consumers'. It was not generosity; it was intentional manipulation. He wanted to create a group of young leaders who were dependent on him; who were literally *eating out of his hand*.

Satan similarly uses culture. He attempts to seduce us with the best it can offer: money, sex, power, fame, food, and entertainment. 'Come and indulge!' he calls. 'Come and satisfy your every desire!' What he wants from us is our compliance. He hopes that we will immerse ourselves in the pleasure our world promises and so be unthinkingly swept along in its value system. He wants us to *go with the flow.* 'Don't be different. Don't rock the boat. Don't stand apart.'

We are not saying our culture is evil; much about it is good. Many of the things used to seduce us are not *bad* things; many of them are *good* things. It is not a sin to engage with them. We praise God for the day Ben met Jerry! We thank God for entertainment, sports and shopping.[28] These things are not in themselves evil. But herein lies the problem: *the things that we start to consume so often begin to consume us.*

What Is Consuming You?

A great question we can ask ourselves is: 'What have I been consuming recently, that has started to consume me?' The answer may be different for each of us.

When we identify these things it can be so helpful to follow Daniel's example, and step away from them. Not necessarily forever (although sometimes this is appropriate) but for a season. 'Abstinence' is a pretty unpopular word in our world, but for the last two thousand years it has been a normal part of following Jesus. It's called fasting.

---

28   For clarification: just internet shopping. Neither of us enjoy real life shopping.

One friend of ours, Laura, is very into fashion. That's not a bad thing; it's a good thing! But Laura began to notice that an awful lot of her time, money and emotional energy was being spent on clothes. It made her uncomfortable. She felt God gently nudging her to 'fast' for a time from clothes shopping. She decided that if she needed anything she would, for a year, shop exclusively at charity shops. She would be the first to say that it was good for her heart.

For some of us it may be that social media has begun to consume us. We might be vaguely aware it has been designed by an evil genius bent on making sure we procrastinate, but we use it anyway. We sit down for a moment, post something, check the likes, check again, like something else etc., etc. Twenty minutes later we leave the public bathroom and look innocently at the waiting queue.

—————————— ANDY ——————————

My problem is with Netflix. I find box sets addictive. The first episode ends, and then the countdown automatically appears:

Next episode starts in 10 …

9 …

8 …

'Where is the controller?'

7 …

6 …
5 …

'I'm sure it was under this cushion!'
4 …
3 …

'Help me!!!'
2 …

'Nooooo!'
1 …

'New episode? Oh well, I've started so I'll finish.'

It has been said that whatever demands our mind's attention and our heart's affection is what we worship. The feeding of our every desire seems a small thing at first; everyone else is doing it. After a while, however, we begin to find that there are certain things we can't do without. They have been designed to suck us in and without knowing it we have become dependent upon them. They begin to demand our unquestioning obedience. Before we know it, sex, not God, is in charge of our lives; or money, not God, is calling the shots; or fame, not God, is our master. The best way to stop something consuming us is to stop consuming it! In

It has been said that whatever demands our mind's attention and our heart's affection, that is what we worship

other words to step back and fast; to rededicate our time, energy, money to our true Lord.

Milk for Jesus

Stepping *back* without completely stepping *out* of our culture is a difficult line to tread. It is not always as clear-cut as fasting. Daniel's resolve not to eat the food was a risky move. When he asked Ashpenaz, the chief eunuch, for only vegetables and water Ash's reply was, 'You've got to be joking, they could cut my head off!' (Dan. 1:10). At this point, if we were Daniel, we would have said, 'Oh well, I tried. OK, could you pass the fillet and fries. I'd hate for you to be killed on my account.'[29] Instead, Daniel negotiated with his guard and suggested a ten-day trial. Drawing a line in the sand was not straightforward for Daniel; he had to work out what it might look like. We also have to tread the high-wire of being involved in our friends' lives but knowing where the line is.

ANDY

At university I played a lot of sport. After a little while I was invited to become a member of the sports drinking society in my college. Lots of my friends were in the society and I really wanted to be

---

29   One of the authors has been saying this in restaurants for years.

involved in their lives – it would have been hard to do this without being around them! So I decided to join.

Inevitably, because it was a 'drinking society' there was a lot of drinking involved! I made it clear that I would love to join the group, but that as a Christian, whilst I might have a pint, I wouldn't be getting drunk. People were okay with this but they insisted I do the initiation that all new members had to go through. This initiation involved various drinking challenges, lasted hours, and usually had people drunk within the first thirty minutes. I had a problem!

Eventually I suggested that I do the initiation alongside the other new recruits, but with milk rather than alcohol. They seemed to take this 'milk initiation' as a challenge, and agreed with a gleam in their eyes. Within minutes of arriving at the initiation I was made to drink several pints of milk. This was the warm-up. By the twenty-minute mark I was throwing up. It became a three-hour milk-endurance test from hell.

For anyone interested, milk when regurgitated has the consistency of cottage cheese. I know this because I studied it in detail as it poured repeatedly from my insides. Of course the other inductees were also vomiting in bushes and nearby bins – they just had the advantage of being completely drunk whilst they were doing it. For the following hours I drank and reproduced milk, all the while competing in various colourful challenges from the beep test to drinking blended raw meat. By the end of the afternoon I'd been put off dairy for life. But I was a stone-cold-sober new member of a drinking society.

Daniel understood that seemingly small decisions have big implications. After the ten-day trial on vegetables and water Daniel and his friends were inspected. 'They looked healthier and better nourished than any of the young men who ate the royal food' (1:15). Our diet dictates our health! Daniel would ask us, 'What do you stop yourself doing because you are a follower of Jesus? What are you refusing to feed your soul with?' Making wise decisions *strengthens us spiritually*. We end up in a far healthier place than those who simply eat without thinking.

Daniel's willingness to draw lines in the sand meant that he was able to learn the language and literature of the Babylonians but his soul didn't feed on it. He became the head of the magicians but stayed faithful to God. He never used their magic, instead relying on his Lord to speak. Daniel didn't dismiss Babylonian culture as 'pure evil' – he was involved at the very centre of power for decades. He spoke God's truth to the highest in the land. This was only possible, however, because his loyalty wasn't compromised; he belonged to his God.

Attack Two: Intimidation

If seduction doesn't work, the next attack is intimidation. Not every attempt to draw a line in the sand will be met with understanding. When we challenge the culture around us and publicly proclaim the good news of Jesus we *will* face opposition. In fact Jesus promised us nothing less, saying to his disciples: 'In this world you will have trouble. But take heart! I have overcome the world' (John 16:33). If seduction attacks our desires, intimidation attacks our fears. When we do stand apart, we won't be warmly invited to conform; we'll be pressured to do so.

The Three Amigos

In Daniel chapter three we read the story of Daniel's three friends. King Neb made an enormous image of gold and ordered everyone to worship it. The Jews refused. 'Furious with rage, Nebuchadnezzar summoned Shadrach, Meshach and Abednego' (Dan. 3:13). He threatened them, ordering them to worship the statue or be burned alive. Their reply to the fearsome tyrant was impressive: 'Shadrach, Meshach and Abednego replied to him, "King Nebuchadnezzar, we do not need to defend ourselves before you in this matter. If we are thrown into the blazing furnace, the God we serve is able to deliver us from it, and he will deliver us from Your Majesty's hand. But even if he does not, we want you to know, Your Majesty, that we will not serve your gods or worship the image of gold you have set up"' (vv. 6-18).

Neb was so furious he ordered the furnace heated seven times hotter than usual.[30] The friends were thrown into the furnace! Within a moment, though, Neb had leapt to his feet. He saw not three but four men wandering about in the flames as if they were in an air-conditioned room. The fourth person looked like a 'son of the gods.' The king shouted, 'Come out!' and the three amigos strolled back (vv. 19-26). In a touch of class, we're told they didn't even smell of smoke!

---

30   Given that a furnace of mildly warm flames will kill you in seconds, making the flames *even hotter* might not have increased the 'threat level' in quite the way Neb hoped …

As a result Neb somewhat changed his tune:

> Then Nebuchadnezzar said, 'Praise be to the God of
> Shadrach, Meshach and Abednego, who has sent his
> angel and rescued his servants! They trusted in him and
> defied the king's command and were willing to give
> up their lives rather than serve or worship any god except
> their own God. Therefore I decree that the people of any
> nation or language who say anything against the God of
> Shadrach, Meshach and Abednego be cut into pieces and
> their houses be turned into piles of rubble, for no other
> god can save in this way' (vv. 28-29).[31]

This was an extraordinary turn around. The king of Babylon was
now giving a testimony about the faithfulness of the God of the
Jews! This great victory happened at the place where the friends
were willing to give up not only their privileges and rights, but also
their lives.

A 'Though' Faith

Martin Luther King Junior was no stranger to intimidation; he
received regular death threats. Preaching in 1967, he referred to the
story of the three friends. Shadrach, Meshach and Abednego knew
God and were confident in his *ability* to deliver them from the
flames. But Dr King made the point that the deeper lesson is found
in the statement the friends made: '*But even if he does not ...* we

---

31 We wonder whether, *after* we had had been cut into hundreds of pieces, we
would mind terribly if our new bathroom was turned to rubble ...

will not serve your gods or worship the image of gold you have set up' (v. 18). Even if God *didn't* save them, they *still* would not bow down and worship the statue. Dr King declared:

> You see there is what you may call an 'if' faith, and there is a 'though' faith. And the permanent faith, the lasting, the powerful faith is the 'though' faith. Now the 'if' faith says, 'If all goes well; if life is hopeful, prosperous and happy; if I don't have to go to jail; if I don't have to face the agonies and burdens of life; if I'm not ever called bad names because of taking a stand that I feel that I must take; if none of these things happen, then I'll have faith in God, then I'll be alright.' That's the 'if' faith ... There is a 'though' faith, though. And the 'though' faith says 'Though things go wrong; though evil is temporarily triumphant; though sickness comes and the cross looms, nevertheless! I'm gonna believe anyway and I'm gonna have faith anyway ...'[32]

On the same morning he announced, 'I say to you, this morning, that if you have never found something so dear and precious to you that you will die for it, then you aren't fit to live.' Within a year, at the age of 39, Martin Luther King Jr was assassinated. We grow a 'though' faith as we stare defeat, failure, even death in the eyes and still choose to trust in our God.

Of course 'staring defeat in the eyes' is easier said than done. When Dr King faced fierce criticism and plummeting popularity

---

32   Martin Luther King, Jr, 'But if not', sermon preached at Ebenezer Baptist Church, Atlanta, Georgia, 5 November 1967.

because of his stance against the Vietnam War, he wrote of his internal battle. He was tempted to compromise, to take the easy option, but ultimately concluded,

> On some positions, Cowardice asks the question, 'Is it safe?' Expediency asks the question, 'Is it politic?' And Vanity comes along and asks the question, 'Is it popular?' But Conscience asks the question, 'Is it right?' And there comes a time when one must take a position that is neither safe, nor politic, nor popular, but he must do it because Conscience tells him it is right ... The ultimate measure of a man is not where he stands in moments of convenience, but where he stands in moments of challenge, moments of great crisis and controversy.[33]

Worth Dying For

Daniel faced a similar test to his three friends (Dan. 6). Years later, when a new king, Darius, occupied the throne, the court officials conspired against Daniel. They convinced the king to issue an edict stating no one was allowed to pray to anyone except him for thirty days. Daniel read this decree, returned home, opened his windows so the city could watch, and *prayed to God*. He continued as he had always done. This is an astonishing act. Daniel would have known

---

33   Martin Luther King, Jr, *The Autobiography of Martin Luther King, Jr.* (Abacus, 2000) 342, 344.

it was a death sentence; however his loyalty to God was more important to him than his own life. As a result he was thrown into a pit of hungry lions. Fortunately, at this point God sent his rescue angel on another mission. Daniel was saved, the tables were turned, and the scheming officials became cat food. Daniel and his three friends had found something so precious they were willing to die for it.

ANDY

I was recently talking with a top Christian businessman who asked me a simple question: 'What are you prepared to die for?' He insisted that I should figure out my answer. He told me it would give me tremendous strength in life and leadership because strength flows from knowing what your non-negotiables are. It's this that means when our back is against the wall, when everything feels confusing, and when we can feel the Enemy's breath on our neck, we know where we stand.

As followers of Jesus we might all say, 'I would die for Jesus.' But understanding what this looks like in the arenas we live in is worth thinking through. Most of the stands we take will not be literal life-or-death moments. They may, however, involve dying a day at a time to our wanting to play it safe, keep everyone happy or run with the crowd. Nor will we necessarily be standing *against* something. Many of the ways God will ask us to stand out will be

It can be helpful to think through: 'What is so important to me that I won't budge, even if it costs me everything?'

by positively standing *for* something.

We can change the atmosphere of our communities simply by living in the opposite spirit. When the atmosphere is full of greed, be generous. If it is full of vindictiveness, speak encouragement. If it is full of sexual promiscuity and using others for our gain, choose to live a life of purity. Finally, in a world that demands its rights, we are to be clear we have a higher calling – loving people as Jesus has loved us. It can be helpful to think through: 'What is so important to me that I won't budge, even if it costs me everything?'

Taking a Stand

One friend of ours, Gary, became a Christian after running a successful company for years. He began to ask how his work could reflect his relationship with God. Eventually he decided that the company would begin to give away ten percent of its profits each year. He also made the decision that they would not open their shops on Sundays. We are not suggesting that all companies run by Christians should do this; the point is that these things became, for him, non-negotiables before God. They were a positive way of him expressing his trust in and dependence upon his heavenly Father.

Over the years he has faced tremendous pressure to compromise – the business community thinks he is crazy. He misses out on a huge amount of Sunday trade; at times the busiest shopping days of the year have fallen on Sundays. Despite this, he would rather resign and close the company than compromise. He is clear that these decisions, and the statement they make to God, his staff and his customers, are worth the cost. As it happens, his business has grown exponentially; he now has over one hundred stores and employs 1,400 people. We know, however, that *even if* that were not the case, he still would not back down.

Two friends of ours, John and Debby, planted a church fourteen years ago. From the beginning they were very clear about what they felt God was calling them to do: they were to preach the gospel and serve the poor. One of the ways this worked itself out is that they committed from the very start to giving away twenty percent of their church's income to causes that didn't benefit the church. Again, we are not suggesting all churches should do this, it is simply that for our friends this became a non-negotiable. During the 2008 financial crisis the great temptation was to compromise – giving to charities was plummeting and their income forecasts we not promising. Instead they felt God telling them to *increase* the church's giving to twenty-two percent. Their backs against the wall, they obeyed. They knew what they stood for. Recently, the church raised millions for a new building project; twenty-two percent of what they raised was not spent on the building but has been invested in ways that benefit the community. During a meeting with the local councillors the church said they would like to give one hundred thousand pounds to help those who are worst off in the locality; it was up to the council how the money was spent. Over the last fourteen years the church has given away over two million pounds. In the middle of a culture that says 'look after number one,' they have made a conscious decision to be generous. They are not afraid to stand out.

Another friend, David, worked temporarily in an office where there was definitely an 'office atmosphere'. Everyone talked about each other behind their backs; the sarcasm had a cutting edge. Our friend hated it and prayed that he would soon find another job. To his surprise he sensed the Lord say to him, 'I've put you here to change the culture.' Our friend began to pray for everyone in the office. As he was praying the Lord instructed him to buy them all chocolates! He arrived early one morning and hid the chocolates in various places. He also hid a box in his own desk. He then left and arrived back with all the other members of the team. Soon someone opened their drawer and exclaimed, 'There's a box of chocolates in here, who put that in there?' Nobody knew. A few minutes later, someone else found a box under their paperwork. Our friend feigned equal surprise as he 'found' his own box of chocolates. Before the morning was over everyone had received a secret gift. Amazingly, the atmosphere completely changed. Everyone started to be nice to one another. (What else could they do? No one wanted to risk being rude to the person who had bought them chocolates.)

What will we stand for in our school? In our family? In our community? What sorts of lives will we decide to live, irrespective of our fears and the pressures that we'll face? We don't know what your pit of lions is, or your

Babylon tried to change Daniel; it failed. Instead, he changed Babylon

blazing furnace, but we do know that deciding in advance, 'I will love, pray, be generous, forgive and be obedient to God, regardless of the consequences' is how we make an impact in our culture. At the beginning of our story Daniel had his Hebrew name changed to Belteshazzar (1:7). By the end of the story, however, the rulers of Babylon were calling him by his own name (5:12; 6:5, 20). Babylon tried to change Daniel; it failed. Instead, he changed Babylon.

Our Secret Weapon

What enabled our heroes to stand firm through the seduction and intimidation?

What gave them their determination? What was it that put that steel in them?

It was a high view of God's loving power. How we see God determines how we behave in this world.

They would not worship the gods of Babylonian culture because they trusted in both the character and might of the God of Israel. How big is your God? Do you see him as a pet poodle that will fetch a pair of slippers for you? Do you see him as a sweet, doting granddad who will give you anything you want? Or do you see him as a strong father who loves you and knows what he is doing?

Daniel didn't think he was in Babylon simply because Neb had a big army. The way he saw it, 'the Lord gave Jehoiakim king of Judah into his hand' (1:2). Daniel saw that God was somehow at work through events. Shadrach, Meshach and Abednego, when faced with the furious Neb, refused to defend themselves. In an amazing way they were stating, 'King Neb, you don't have power over us, our God does – he's the one really in control.' Daniel's great prayer in chapter 9 is a cry to God to take them back to the land of Israel – it is based on a belief and confidence in God's power to do so. His visions in chapters 7-12 are hard to understand but rest on the foundational belief that God has the final say on the future. This deep conviction is seen throughout the book of Daniel.

Where did Daniel and his friends get this confidence from?

It's one thing to hear God's promises; it's another to trust God's promises

It developed because of their relationship with God. They spent time with him – Daniel prayed three times a day. They heard from him – much of Daniel's book is filled with visions God gave him. And they trusted in his Word. There is a wonderful promise that was sent to the Israelites whilst they were in exile in Babylon: 'This is what the Lord says: "When seventy years are completed for Babylon, I will come to you and fulfil my good promise to bring you back to this place. For I know the plans I have for you," declares the LORD, "plans to prosper you and not to harm you, plans to give you hope and a future"' (Jer. 29:10-11).

It's one thing to hear God's promises; it's another to *trust* God's promises. Daniel and the boys knew that God would ultimately have his way. When we really believe that God is in control of the future, we are able to take a stand in the present. It's impossible to overstate how differently we live when we are convinced that our God wins.

The Final Whistle

MIKE

I have been a Manchester United fan since 1968. One high point of my life was meeting Jesus. The other high point came in 1999 when United won the Treble. We won the Premiership, we won the FA Cup and then we played Bayern Munich at the Camp Nou stadium in Barcelona for the Champions League. Loads of people went to the pub to watch it. I didn't – it was too important for me. I had to be on my own in my house, kneeling in front of the TV, praying and fasting. I was desperately anxious that the dream would be fulfilled!

The match did not go well. Bayern Munich outplayed us and after a while the inevitable happened – they scored. They then started repeatedly hitting the post and were close to scoring a second time. I was fretful, hopeless and despairing. I'm embarrassed to say there were times I was on the verge of tears.

We clung on until the last minute of normal time. Then United got a corner. David Beckham went to take it. The commentator said, '*Can United score? They always score …*' Beckham took the corner; it was headed out. Someone kicked it back in and it came to Teddy Sheringham. Teddy swivelled round and helped it into the net. Everyone went crazy!

I was thinking, 'It'll be extra time. They've been playing better than us. We'll probably lose it.' We were in time added on. Then United broke. The ball came in from the left. Ole Gunnar Solskjaer, my hero, slid in and put it into the back of the net! I was delirious with joy. I was screaming and shouting. My mourning turned into dancing.

That ninety minutes nearly killed me. I never want to go through that again. But after it was over I went out and bought the DVD. Now, whenever I have a bad day or am feeling low, I'll go home and watch the match from the kick-off. They play the same as they did in the original. United don't play well. Bayern score. Bayern hit the woodwork. It's

Do you know how it's going to end? Have you looked at the back of the Bible? Jesus wins and we win with him

horrible. But I'm not anxious. I'm smiling. I'm enjoying it because I know how it's going to end. Solskjaer is going to put it in the back of the net with virtually the last kick of the match. I know that from the beginning.

Do you know how it's going to end? Have you looked at the back of the Bible? Jesus wins and we win with him. Daniel's trust in God's loving supremacy enabled him to stand firm in a culture that threatened to sweep him off of his feet. Christian hope is much more than wishful thinking. It is a decision to live in the midst of our world engaged and caring, whilst knowing that this is not all there is. God is at work – he is both good, and the ruler of the future.

Changing a World

Five hundred and fifty years after Daniel, Jesus was born.

During those 550 years, Satan's tactics hadn't changed.

First he tried seduction. Satan came to Jesus in the wilderness and offered him all the kingdoms of the world. It might seem like generosity; it was, in fact, manipulation. Satan wanted Jesus eating out of his hand. Jesus (who was fasting at the time) refused.

Next, Satan opted for all-out intimidation – death threats; the threat of the cross. Jesus looked squarely at the cross and, trusting in his Father, resolutely went to meet his fate. The commands of his Father were precious enough to die for. Unlike Daniel and the three friends, Jesus was not snatched from his execution at the last possible moment. He truly had a 'though' faith. Like many of those who have since followed him, he was put to death. He was humiliated; made to look utterly foolish in the eyes of a world that did not understand who he was living for. Jesus, however, still decided to give up his life. His love for his God and his world far outweighed his desire for self-preservation.

Jesus' obedience paved a way for the kingdom of heaven to be established in our world. They tried to change Jesus and yet, two thousand years later, two billion Christians point to the truth that Jesus has changed the world! Three days after he entered his 'blazing furnace', the impossible happened. Jesus was raised from the dead – a living testimony to the fact that ultimately God's ending is the only one that will be written.

Be loyal to God. Depend on him alone. Know what he has called you to. Do it regardless of the consequences. Believe he writes the ending. And watch what happens.

Read Daniel's Lifeline for Yourself

Daniel's book tells the account of his life and records the visions he received from God. Some of the key events are:

- Daniel and his friends are captured and brought to Babylon, Daniel 1
- The three friends are thrown into the blazing furnace, Daniel 3
- Daniel is thrown into the lions' den, Daniel 6

- Daniel prays for God to have mercy, and to act on behalf of the Jews, Daniel 9
- Daniel has a series of visions, Daniel 7-12

Group questions

1. Can you name some of the ways in which our culture attempts to seduce you? Which is the most successful?

2. Can you name some of the ways the world around you attempts to intimidate you? Which of these is the most successful?

3. Can you name your equivalent to Daniel's refusal to eat the food of the Babylonians? (Clue: it often has something to do with money, sex or power.)

4. Can you name a time you were placed in the equivalent of a blazing furnace or a den of lions for your faith? How did it work out?

5. What decisions can you make now that will help you to not compromise your beliefs in the months and years ahead?

6. Do you know what your non-negotiables are? Your lines in the sand? Those things you are willing to 'die' for?

CHAPTER 7

SIN, SWEETNESS AND DEATH: LESSONS FROM THE LIFE OF SAMSON

And lead us not into temptation.

Matthew 6:13

 MIKE

I was about to go out for the evening when I remembered that I had guests arriving for lunch the next day and no dessert ready for them. I looked in my freezer and found a double chocolate cake saved for emergencies such as this. I removed the packaging and placed the chocolate cake in the fridge where it would defrost slowly. I then left for my evening out. I returned late that night and went into the kitchen to drink a glass of water before bed. As I was standing in the kitchen I wondered how the double chocolate cake was doing defrosting in the fridge. I decided to go and have a look, resolving that I would not taste the cake as I had already eaten my evening meal and I like to watch my figure. When I opened the fridge door, something happened which was both unexpected and shocking. The double chocolate cake spoke to me!

'Hello Mike,' it said, 'how are you this evening?'

I replied out of politeness, 'Fine thank you. I am a little weary so I'm just going to bed.'

Then, out of pastoral concern, I asked, 'And how are you tonight?'

The cake gave a long sigh, looked at me with those big chocolate buttons and said, 'OK I suppose. To be honest I am lonely and bored in this fridge. I only have a cucumber and two tomatoes for company. I have a suggestion. You are tired, I am bored. Why don't you take me out of the fridge, put me on the table, and we can both unwind and converse while you finish your glass of water. Then you can pop me back in the fridge and go to bed.

This suddenly seemed like a good idea. After all, I reasoned, there is nothing in the Bible that says you can't talk to double chocolate cakes. 'I will do that on the clear understanding that we will just talk. I won't eat you though, as I have already had my dinner and I want to save you for tomorrow's lunch.'

'Absolutely,' said the cake, 'a little chat and then bed.' The way the cake said 'bed' sent a shiver up my spine. My hands became clammy and I suddenly felt hot. I suppose I should have seen the warning signs.

Partly to make conversation and partly because I was curious, I asked, 'Tell me Cakey,' (I felt I could be more informal as by now we were developing a friendship), 'are you defrosted yet? I hope you don't think I am being forward in asking.'

'Not at all,' responded Cakey. 'I think I am defrosted but I can't be sure. The only way we can find out is if you run your finger along my cream and have a lick.'

I kept looking at Cakey's cream and the more I looked the more beautiful it seemed. I imagined the cream in my mouth exploding my taste buds.

'I shouldn't eat you,' I said weakly.

'Oh come on,' responded Cakey, 'we are just talking about a lick. This is the twenty-first century for goodness' sake.'

Suddenly Cakey's words seemed so reasonable and I thought that licking Cakey's cream was not technically going all the way. Anyway, I suddenly needed to know before lunch the next day whether we were compatible. So I did it. It was everything I imagined it to be and so much more. I felt alive in a way I had never known before.

'Cakey,' I blurted out before I could stop to think, 'your cream is defrosted, but what I desperately need to know is this: are you defrosted deep, deep in the heart of you?'

There was only one way to find out. I resolved to only take one small slice, a mere slither. However, on that fateful night, one thing led to another, and by the end of the evening that double chocolate cake and I were one flesh. I wish I could report that I hated every minute of it, but I loved every mouthful. As I was eating Cakey I became indignant at all the dieticians who kept telling me that eating a whole double chocolate cake on your own in one sitting is bad for your health. 'What do they know?' I reasoned. 'How can something that feels so right be so wrong? Cakey and I love each other and all I am doing is expressing that love.'

And then Cakey was gone. I looked at the empty plate, the spoon and the knife smeared with Cakey's remains and I suddenly felt sick. And thirsty. Oh, so very thirsty. That night I hardly slept.

That's the trouble with sin. It feels good at the time but later it repeats on you and you feel sick. Where did I go wrong? I went wrong when I opened the fridge door. Don't open the fridge door! When we do it is often too late.

Don't open the fridge door! When we do it is often too late

Many of us long to serve Jesus with our whole hearts and lives and be used by him to make a difference in this world. Probably the major stumbling block to our achieving this is that we are distracted, damaged and defeated by giving in to the temptation to sin. Sin is not a trendy word but it is a 'Bible word' and in this chapter we will look at the nature of sin, the destructiveness of sin and the consequences of giving in to sin. We will also look at how we can put things in place so we can live healthy lives free from the grip of sin. To help us we're going to spend some time with someone who is an example of *what not to do.*

The Tragedy of Samson

Samson's story can be found in the book of Judges chapters 13 to 16. There are some strange aspects to the story which are difficult to understand. One thing is crystal clear, however, and that is Samson's failure. His disobedience and unwillingness to make healthy decisions led to his enslavement to his lusts and passions. Samson's tale is one of excess, a complete lack of self-control and, as a result, a ruined life. His story is a tragedy.

The story begins brightly enough. An angel was sent to Samson's mother to tell her she would have a baby. She was told, 'the boy is to be a Nazirite, dedicated to God from the womb. He will take the lead in delivering Israel from the hands of the Philistines' (Judg. 13:5). Nazirites were those who made special vows to God. Often this would be just for a season; a little like people giving up chocolate in the run up to Easter but slightly more intense![34] You can read about the Nazirite vow in Numbers 6. There were three key aspects:

1. Nazirites were not allowed to drink wine or alcohol of any kind. This was taken to an apparent extreme. They were not allowed to have anything to do with vines – no eating of grapes or raisins – they were even explicitly warned not to eat the *skin* of a grape (Num. 6:1-4).[35]

2. During the period of their dedication Nazirites were not to cut their hair but were instructed to let it grow long. When we think of long hair today we can think of shimmering straight hair, or beautiful springy curls. The Nazirites, however, lived before the age of hair-straighteners and frizz-

---

34   Mike is not sure it can get much more 'intense' than giving up chocolate.

35   If you are wondering why anyone would *want* to eat the skin of a grape, so are we …

ease, so picture instead a giant bird's nest. Their huge, wild, crazy hair would have been symbolic of their lives dedicated to God. They were outrageously and obviously set apart for him (Num. 6:5).

3. Nazirites were not allowed to go near a dead body. This was so strict that they were told that even if a member of their family died they were to keep away from the body. It would have made funeral attendance problematic (Num. 6:6-12).

The Nazirite vow was serious business! Samson was to be a Nazirite *from birth*; he was never to go near a grape, a barber or a dead body. The promise alongside this was that he would become one of the leaders of his people and free them from their enemies.

Pushing the Limits

Throughout his life Samson pushed the limits of his vows. Once, on the way to visit a girl he wanted to marry, he wandered through some vineyards (Judg. 14:5). What was Samson doing approaching vineyards when he knew that living as a Nazirite meant keeping away? Perhaps he justified it to himself: 'There is no wine there, only grapes and I'm not going to eat any. God will not take his anointing away just because I am walking near a grapevine.'

As Samson walked through the vineyard a lion attacked him. Filled with the Spirit of God, Samson used superhuman strength to kill the lion. This supernatural strength became his trademark gift. It meant that despite their efforts, the Philistines could not defeat or trap him. However Samson used his gift in an angry and petulant way. He killed Philistines out of hatred and revenge. The battles he fought were not to help Israel, but to serve himself.

Time passed and Samson returned to the vineyard (v. 8). He decided to turn aside and look at the carcass of the dead lion. Bees had made a nest inside the body and Samson noticed the honey. He could not resist. The honey looked so sweet. 'It can't be that bad,' he must have reasoned, 'It is only honey. If I bend my hand a certain way I will barely be touching the lion carcass.' He opened the fridge door and broke the second of the vows.

Samson mistook God's patient love for approval of his actions

At this point Samson's strength had not left him; he still had his anointing. He would no doubt have been relieved, and therefore justified his actions.: 'God is still with me. He is still using me. He clearly doesn't mind that I have bent the rules a little.' Samson mistook God's patient love for approval of his actions. A terrible error to make! Instead of repenting in humility Samson was puffed up with pride. What he hadn't seen were the warning signs: he might have been the strongest person on the planet, but he was vulnerable.

My, My, My Delilah

Samson's desires repeatedly ruled him. He insisted on marrying a Philistine against the advice and counsel of his parents. When his new wife displeased him he discarded her. Next he found a prostitute and slept with her. Finally, he met Delilah and fell head over heels.

Delilah clearly didn't feel the same way. The rulers of the Philistines quietly offered her money; they wanted to find out the source of Samson's strength in order to destroy him. She asked him (probably over a candle-lit meal one evening) "Tell me the secret of your great strength and how you can be tied up and subdued." Samson answered her, "If anyone ties me with seven fresh bowstrings that have not been dried, I'll become as weak as any other man." (Judg. 16:6-7).

Delilah got the bowstrings and tied Samson up. Hidden in the room were Philistine soldiers. 'Samson, the Philistines are upon you!' she cried. Samson snapped the bowstrings easily, and defeated his enemies."

Delilah then said, 'You have made a fool of me; you lied to me. Come now, tell me how you can be tied.' At this point Samson should have said, 'You must be nuts if you think I'm going to tell you after *that*! You just tied me up and invited the Philistine army over to murder me. I'm afraid it's not working out between us Delilah. It's not me, it's you ...'

Instead Samson told her another version of the same lie. In his arrogance he thought he could play around even with this vow and still avoid consequences. The scenario repeated itself yet again. Finally, we read:

> Then she said to him, 'How can you say, "I love you," when you won't confide in me? This is the

third time you have made a fool of me and haven't told me the secret of your great strength.' With such nagging she prodded him day after day until he was sick to death of it.

So he told her everything. 'No razor has ever been used on my head,' he said, 'because I have been a Nazirite dedicated to God from my mother's womb. If my head were shaved, my strength would leave me, and I would become as weak as any other man.'

When Delilah saw that he had told her everything, she sent word to the rulers of the Philistines, 'Come back once more; he has told me everything.' So the rulers of the Philistines returned with the silver in their hands. After putting him to sleep on her lap, she called for someone to shave off the seven braids of his hair, and so began to subdue him. And his strength left him.

Then she called, 'Samson, the Philistines are upon you!'

He awoke from his sleep and thought, 'I'll go out as before and shake myself free.' But he did not know that the LORD had left him. Then the Philistines seized him, gouged out his eyes and took him down to Gaza. (Judg. 16:15-21)

A short time later the Philistines threw a party in the temple of their god to celebrate Samson's defeat. They had Samson brought in to entertain them, not realising that his hair had begun to grow again. Samson asked a servant to guide him to the pillars that held up the roof. He cried out to God one last time, 'Then he pushed with all his might, and down came the temple on the rulers and all the people in it. Thus he killed many more when he died than while he lived' (v. 30).

This final 'victory' was a hollow one; it spoke only of what *might have been* had Samson pursued God faithfully. He had been uniquely gifted and yet, for all his potential, his near total lack of self-control set him on a one-way path to self-destruction.

What are the lessons we can learn from Samson's tragedy?

The RSVP

God's calling comes with an RSVP. And how we respond matters.

In the words of JK Rowling: 'It is our choices … that show what we truly are, far more than our abilities.'[36] Samson had enormous ability; he was more than capable of fulfilling his destiny; however, he was not a robot. He could make choices that would either enable him to walk into God's

> *God's calling comes with an RSVP. And how we respond matters*

---

36   JK Rowling, *Harry Potter and the Chamber of Secrets* (Bloomsbury Publishing, 2014) 352.

plan or kill him. The same is true of us. We, like Samson, have a great calling. Jesus invites us to partner with him in the building of his kingdom. Our choices, however, play a crucial role in this. If, rather than rejecting his Nazirite vows, Samson had embraced them, his story would have been very different.

What might a modern-day Nazirite look like?

So often in the Old Testament, physical laws point to spiritual truths. Today we are not banned from having a haircut, but we do want to be set apart. We want our spiritual hair to grow long; to refuse to 'cut short' our whole-hearted devotion to God. We want to be marked out by our crazy obedience; our wild willingness to follow our saviour on great adventures!

We want to be marked out by our crazy obedience, our wild willingness to follow our saviour on great adventures!

We achieve this in part by a ruthless obedience to the principles behind the two other vows. The vow about alcohol does not mean we cannot have a glass of wine. The spiritual principle is that we are to avoid coming under the influence of anything that would intoxicate us and take away our power to make good decisions as we follow God. Equally, the vow about avoiding dead bodies does not mean we should Facetime into Grandma's funeral from a safe distance. Rather, we are to refuse to touch anything that kills us spiritually. If it harms or damages our relationship with God, we aren't to go near it.

Do we want to live lives of openhearted, radical, risk-taking obedience to God?

If the answer is YES – yes to loving him, serving him, following him – then this one, mighty YES leads, unavoidably, to a thousand other NOs. If God had invited us to a party, with date and location set, and we had RSVP'd 'We'll be there', then this would mean turning down any other invitation that clashed. Our YES to God means we will live lives saying *no* to other things. The underlying heart behind the Nazirite vows was saying YES to God. The way this YES worked itself out was through the three nos – no to alcohol, haircuts, and corpses.

> *Our YES to God means we will live lives saying no to other things*

Whilst our YES may be one, big, momentary decision, it is lived out in hundreds and thousands of small daily choices. These choices matter. They reveal who we are, and shape who we will become. They will often involve saying *no*. They are an essential part of walking into our calling. As such, it's best to be as clued up as possible when making them.

Here's what Samson probably wished he had known …

Deceitful Delilah

When we are playing an opponent in a high-stakes match we want to understand their game plan. What are they going to throw at us? What tactics will they use? When it comes to enticing us away from God and towards sin, Satan's tactics are simple. We use them to catch mice, fish, and restaurant customers. The cheese in the trap, the worm on the hook, the free sample on the cocktail stick. In a word: bait.

Temptation begins with the offer of honey. When Adam and Eve first looked at the forbidden fruit they saw that it was 'good for food and pleasing to the eye' (Gen. 3:6). If the fruit had been rotten and mouldy they would never have taken it. If Mike's friend had been Cabbagey instead of Cakey he wouldn't have bothered 'checking in' when he got home. This is the first thing to understand about sin: we will *want* to do it. The second thing to understand is what happens when we do.

Sin looks delightful, but it is deceitful. It promises us life, but in the end it delivers only death. Paul writes: 'the wages of sin is death' (Rom. 6:23). The honey in the lion's carcass is a perfect picture of temptation and sin. It was something sweet inside of something dead! The very same picture repeats itself with Delilah and the Philistines. She is lovely, appealing, charming – the bait – sitting in the middle of a room of murderous Philistines – the trap. Sweetness wrapped in death. This is always the way sin works.

> *Sin looks delightful, but it is deceitful. It promises us life, but in the end it delivers only death*

In CS Lewis' *The Lion, the Witch and the Wardrobe*, one of the four children, Edmund, gets separated from the others in Narnia.[37] He bumps into the White Witch. She seems friendly at first, asking him what he would most like to eat. His favourite sweet is Turkish Delight; the witch obliges and Edmund thinks he's hit the jackpot! As he shovels Turkish Delight into his mouth the witch begins to ask him questions about his siblings; she has an evil plan to trap them. Edmund, meanwhile, finds the more Turkish Delight he eats, the more he wants. Eventually, he is lured into betraying his family for a box of sweets.

'How ridiculous!' we might think, 'I'd never betray my mum for a *Mars bar*!' Edmund, however, didn't begin by betraying his family; he began by eating Turkish Delight that he *thought* was a free gift. Once he was hooked, he couldn't help himself. If only he'd realised the sweetness came with death attached. Whenever Satan tempts us, it begins with 'free samples' to get us hooked. It feels good to be greedy, lose our temper or gossip about someone. We might think that when we've tasted this once, we would be satisfied. But the more we indulge, the more we want to indulge. The more we sin, the more we want to sin. Eventually we find ourselves turning our backs on God's will, because there is something else we want more. We are lured into abandoning our almighty loving Father for the equivalent of a box of sweets.

Don't be fooled by Delilah! She is seductively, gently, intimately leading you towards your destruction. The Bible has a lot to say about sex (try Song of Songs). It celebrates it, but also says the

---

37   Mike: I woke up this morning to find a lion AND a witch in my wardrobe. When I asked them what they were doing, they shouted, 'Narnia business!' Andy: I apologise. Mike does the footnotes.

context for it is marriage. This is one area that has trapped many Christians. Pornography is an example of the way sin works.

When someone begins watching pornography, it starts as something seemingly desirable and harmless. Very soon, the porn they began watching does not satisfy and the person has to go looking for more. Gradually, without the person realising, an addiction can develop. The more they watch it, the more they want to watch it. It starts as something 'sweet' but it leads to a place of death. The 'death' surrounding pornography is huge: it literally rewires our brain. It causes us to treat people as objects. We misunderstand the relationship between sex and intimacy and so struggle to have healthy relationships. We also unknowingly feed a huge, global sex-trafficking industry. In addition to this we often feel a deep sense of shame and guilt. This shame means we keep our addiction a secret; we don't tell our closest friends and that creates a barrier between them and us. We end up too ashamed to draw close to God and find it difficult to receive his love.

This is not a chapter about pornography; it is simply one of many sins that starts out mildly satisfying and leads somewhere very bad. It is fairly easy to lie, to be unkind, to not care about the suffering in the world around us, to take advantage of others. Yet God tells us our YES to him means no to all these things and more. God tells us this because he is holy; but also because he *loves us*. When we fall into sin, there is, of course, forgiveness. There are also, sadly, as in Samson's story, consequences. Our Father does not want us to head down a smooth, easy, attractive road to destroying our lives. Delilah is deceitful. She does not care about you; she is tricking you. The moment she can spring her trap, she will.

Spotting Our Patterns

Samson must have known, on some level, that Delilah was tricking him, but he kept on dating her. Even after we have realised something is killing us spiritually, many of us can't just walk away. Paul the great apostle knew what this was like. He wrote, 'I do not understand what I do ... For I do not do the good I want to do, but the evil I do not want to do – this I keep on doing' (Rom. 7:15, 19). Paul goes on describe a war raging inside of him: he delights in God, but the 'sin living inside' him keeps fighting to enslave him. Most of us can probably relate to the feeling of having an 'inner battle' with temptation. We want to resist, but it's hard.

> *Samson must have known, on some level, that Delilah was tricking him, but he kept on dating her*

One thing that can help is to begin to spot the patterns of sin in our lives. Had Samson reflected on this, he might have noticed that he kept falling for women and shortly afterwards having trouble with Philistines! This happened on three separate occasions: with his wife, a prostitute and then Delilah (Judg. 15-16). Recognising his own pattern of self-destruction would have helped put Samson on his guard. What are your patterns? It can be helpful to ask two questions:

1. *What* sins do I find tempting? It's an obvious thing to point out, but we have different 'Delilahs'. What attracts someone else might not be an issue for us, and vice versa.

2. *When* am I most likely to sin? If we stop to look at those moments we have given into temptation there will probably be a pattern. The two of us have noticed that every year after our summer conferences we are very vulnerable to letting God or ourselves down. The reason for this is a simple one: we are emotionally and physically exhausted. In fact, Alcoholics Anonymous uses an acronym: HALT. It means when you are Hungry, Angry, Lonely or Tired, stop, be aware, you are most likely to mess up at this point. When we are weak, temptation is strong.

Once we've started to notice how and when we are likely to sin, we can begin to break these cycles. It isn't easy, but the Bible offers a pretty clear guide for how to deal with our sin. Paul sums it up in his second letter to Timothy: 'Flee the evil desires of youth and pursue righteousness, faith, love and peace, along with those who call on the Lord out of a pure heart' (2 Tim. 2:22). These two words 'flee' and 'pursue' give us a great approach to beating temptation.[38]

Flee the Fridge

To flee temptation means to run hard in the opposite direction. We often take a more casual approach. We hang around the fridge door,

---

38   Francis Chan makes this point in his talk titled, 'When Sin Looks More Enjoyable Than God', http://crazylove.org/sermon/11.

telling ourselves that we are still in control. Right up until his destruction Samson foolishly thought he was still on top of the situation. His final words before he was captured were: 'I'll go out as before and shake myself free' (Judg. 16:20). How many of us say something similar only to discover too late that we have been trapped?

Had Samson 'fled the fridge' his story might have gone like this: 'Some time later, Samson fell in love with Delilah. As they sat watching their favourite romantic comedy, Delilah turned to Samson. "Hey sweetie, tell me, just theoretically, if I wanted to overpower and destroy you, how might I do that?" "Excuse me a moment, darling!" cried Samson as he leapt off the sofa, dived through a window, and ran for the hills.'

This is not actually as ridiculous as it might sound.

When Joseph was offered sex by Potiphar's wife, his response was much as Samson's should have been: 'though she spoke to Joseph day after day, he refused to go to bed with her or even to be with her. One day he went into the house to attend to his duties, and none of the household servants was inside. She caught him by his cloak and said, "Come to bed with me!" But he left his cloak in her hand and ran out of the house' (Gen. 39:10-12).

Were we advising Joseph we might have said, 'Calm down Joe. Okay, you don't need to sleep with her, but it's fine to be in the same room. You can have a conversation at least; you don't want her to think you're rude.' We're not sure Jesus would have given this advice. Two thousand years ago, Jesus said, 'Don't open the fridge door.' He put it like this: 'If your right eye causes you to stumble, gouge it out and throw it away. It is better for you to lose one part of your body than for your whole body to be thrown into hell. And if your right hand causes you to stumble, cut it off and throw it away. It is better for you to lose one part of your body than for your whole body to go into hell' (Matt. 5:29-30). These are strong words! Jesus is using hyperbole, a rabbinical teaching technique, to make a point. The point is not that we need to literally rip out eyes, it is: be ruthless with the sin in your life. If we are not yet ready to be ruthless when it comes to sin, we are not yet serious enough about it. This is not a popular or fashionable message today, but it is a Biblical one.

Samson became increasingly vulnerable until he was conquered. The lesson for those of us who want to be Nazirites, living exuberantly and wholly dedicated to God, is that licking the cream usually means we go all the way. Saying 'no' means running hard in the *opposite* direction! Understand yourself, know when and by what you are most likely to be tempted, then don't hang around and make friends: flee!

A great friend of ours, Tom, became addicted to pornography at a very early age. When he was nineteen, he became a Christian and, as he puts it, 'the battle began.' Years later he is happily married and free from his addiction, but he is also ruthless when it comes to avoiding certain things. When he goes to the cinema, if the film is rated 12 or above, he will ask the salesperson why that rating has been given. If the attendant replies, 'Because there are some action scenes and things get blown up', Tom will say, 'Great! One ticket please.' He does not find it difficult to resist the temptation towards anger and violence; that is not his particular vice. If, however, the attendant says, 'Because there are some mild sex scenes and a bit of nudity', Tom will say, 'OK scrap that. Give me a ticket for the latest Disney film.' He will not come close to watching anything that could stir up his old habits.

Pursue the King

We might know what we are to run from – envy, lust, anger, greed, jealousy, cruelty, pride, gossip – but what are we to run towards? Paul tells us to run towards 'righteousness, faith, love and peace' (2 Tim. 2:22). Put another way, when we are tempted we are to run *from* sin and *towards* God, in whom righteousness, faith, love and peace are found.

Where Samson failed spectacularly in this Jesus succeeded perfectly. Jesus understands the battles that we face because he has been there before us. He is fully God, and fully human. The writer to the Hebrews says of Jesus: 'For we do not have a high priest who is unable to empathise with our weaknesses, but we have one who has been tempted in every way, just as we are – yet he did not sin' (Heb. 4:15). If anyone ever perfectly fulfilled the spirit of the Nazirite vows, it was Jesus.

In practice, how do we run towards God? If Samson shows us how not to do it, Jesus shows us what we can do.

We Pray

Prayer makes a difference. When we are fighting temptation, it is one of the best weapons we have. Jesus' greatest test was the cross. On the night he was arrested we have an account of his agony in the garden of Gethsemane. The anguish was so painful, we are told that Jesus' sweat was like drops of blood (Luke 22:44). He was battling with his wish to avoid the cross but his desire to fulfil his Father's will. At this moment of desperate need, Jesus prayed. This was his resource; it was what strengthened him.

Jesus also told the disciples with him: 'Watch and pray so that you will not fall into temptation. The spirit is willing, but the flesh is weak' (Matt. 26:41). Most of us can relate to that! We are willing *and* weak. We want to do the right thing, but so often fall short. Jesus commands us to pray!

Prayer, in this sense, just means asking God for help. The moment we cry out to God, the Holy Spirit immediately partners with us. He sees what we want to be free from and he begins to walk that journey with us. He does not remove our choices, those are always our responsibility; but he can strengthen our resolve.

We Hide God's Word in Our Hearts

To prevent capsizing, ships carry extra weight, called ballast.[39] A ship without ballast is likely to be blown over quickly and easily by a slight shift in the wind. God's Word adds 'ballast' to our lives. One psalmist writes of taking on board some of God's truth and explains why: 'I have hidden your word in my heart that I might not sin against you' (Ps. 119:11). When we are full of God's truth, we're far less likely to be deceived by Satan's lies. It gives us stability.

Satan tempted Jesus in the wilderness. Jesus' YES to his Father meant that he replied to Satan's three seemingly attractive offers with three nos. For each no he used the phrase, 'It is written' and quoted Scripture (Matt. 4:1-11). The Scripture was Jesus' guide;

---

39   Mike also does this.

it helped him live free of sin because it showed him what his Father's will for his life was. One of the most important things we can ever do is hide God's truth in our hearts. This is far more than just reading the Bible; it is meditating on it. It is chewing, savouring and digesting it. It is receiving it as the loving, true words of a Father wiser than us and committed to our flourishing. We run towards God by running to his Word.

We Confess

The mistake many of us make after we sin is that we then make things worse by hiding from God! We feel guilt and shame. We wonder whether, if we hide for a few days, someone else nearby will do something worse and God might realise we're not that bad after all.

Sin separates us from God for two reasons. First, God is holy. Holiness and sin don't mix any more than light and darkness. Second, sin comes with shame attached. We are often too ashamed to admit what we've done. Satan also plays his tricks here. As AW Tozer has noted, in the Bible Satan is called the Tempter and the Accuser. He tempts us to sin, then accuses us for doing so! God, however, does not encourage guilt-trips. Jesus did not sin, but he understood that his followers would. In the Lord's Prayer he told his disciples to pray 'lead us not into temptation,' but he also taught them to ask 'forgive us our sins.'

One of the keys to pursuing God is to repent quickly. There is a danger that this sounds like a permission slip to do whatever we want and then throw out a token 'sorry' afterwards. That is not what we are suggesting. That is not true repentance, it is presuming on God's mercy and faithfulness. Instead, what we are saying is that in those moments when we have messed up and we are sorry (we will recognise them), then we need not run *from* God but *towards* him. This is what the lost son finally decided to do in one of Jesus' most famous stories (Luke 15:11-32). He discovered that the moment his father saw him returning in the distance, he sprinted to embrace him. The instant we turn towards God in repentance, he rushes to us. His mercy really is that rich! John put it like this: 'If we confess our sins, he is faithful and just and will forgive us our sins and purify us from all unrighteousness' (1 John 1:9).

Confessing to God is a must. Confessing to each other is also incredibly helpful. Alcoholics Anonymous have another saying: 'You're only as sick as your secrets.' Paul encourages Timothy to 'pursue righteousness, faith, love and peace, *along with those who call on the Lord out of a pure heart*' (2 Tim. 2:22). In other words, pursue God with other people. If we are struggling with something, one of the most important steps we can take is to confess to someone we trust.

──────────── ANDY ────────────

Mike and I have always made a point of confessing to each other when we mess up. It helps us receive God's forgiveness and it frees us from shame. We can speak the truth of God's forgiveness and love to each other. Many years ago when I was a student there was a girl I really fancied. I knew dating her would be a bad idea for all sorts of reasons. Mike was on a diet at the time. We agreed that we would encourage each other. Whenever I was tempted to get in touch with her, I would text Mike. Whenever he was tempted to eat a kebab, he would text me. Mike was once preaching somewhere and at the end of his sermon he had two texts on his phone from me.

The first said: 'I could be texting a beautiful nineteen-year-old girl. Instead, I'm texting an ugly forty-nine-year-old man. My will power is amazing.'

The second (sent twenty minutes after the first), said: 'Oh no! I've just texted her!'

Needless to say a number of jokes were subsequently cracked about my 'amazing' will power!

We Fall in Love

The great secret to living as a modern Nazirite is this: love. Samson's life displays virtually no relationship with his God. He prays only twice: the first time a grumpy request for water and the second for vengeance. In contrast, Jesus regularly retreated into the wilderness to be alone with his Father. Jesus perfectly obeyed his Father, because he perfectly loved him.

The real key to resisting temptation is to be so in love with God that those things which once looked attractive lose their appeal

And he told us, 'Anyone who loves me will obey my teaching' (John 14:23). The real key to resisting temptation is to be so in love with God that those things which once looked attractive lose their appeal. This may sound a little 'airy-fairy' but it is deeply practical.

—————————— ANDY ——————————

When I was growing up, no matter how many times my mum told me to tidy my room, I couldn't do it. I would try for a week or so but then fall back into bad habits. Then something strange happened; I fell in love. Now, whenever my girlfriend came over, the room automatically got tidied. It wasn't an effort; it wasn't something I forced myself to do through gritted teeth — I was happy to do it![40]

I once heard the preacher Joyce Meyer tell a story about a dog called Fred. Fred loved legs. As a result he was kept on a lead. This solved the problem for a while but sooner or later the inevitable would happen – Fred would slip his lead. When he did he would rush to the nearest leg and have his doggy way with it. The solution, Joyce said, was not that Fred needed to be restrained. He needed to be retrained; he needed his desires to be changed. This would mean that even on those occasions when he did slip his lead, he wouldn't chase the legs. Ultimately we, like Fred, need our desires reshaped.

—————

40　Then I got dumped and my room returned to a dump. I think my mum was more upset than I was.

The key is not simply considering how destructive sin is; it is discovering how amazing God is. Saying YES to God means we will be saying no to many other things, but when we understand who we have welcomed into our lives those nos become the easiest decisions in the world. If you want to get better at saying no, become obsessed with your YES. Focus on, delight in and grow in knowledge of your God. Hold before you the One worthy of all your heart, soul, mind and strength. When we truly see his worth, the 'sacrifice' of staying away from sin won't seem a sacrifice. One practical way to do this is to spend time worshipping God – it is to this that our final lifeline speaks.

Read Samson's Lifeline for Yourself

Samson's story is told in Judges 13-16. Key events include:

- His birth foretold and the instructions about Nazirite vows given, Judges13
- His failed marriage and battles with the Philistines, Judges14-15
- His relationship with Delilah and his death, Judges 16

Group questions

1. What do you think of the statement, 'The anointing that is upon you will kill you if the character that is inside you cannot sustain you'?

2. List the practical things you can do to avoid finding yourself in the place where you eat your version of Cakey.

3. Can you name the temptations that you are particularly susceptible to? Why is it important to do this?

4. Do you have someone in your life with whom you can be totally honest about temptations you face? What are the things that might prevent you having this kind of accountability?

5. Do you see the link between loving God and resisting temptation?

6. What do you understand by the word 'repentance'? What does it mean in practise to 'repent'? (Clue: the word literally means 'to turn around'.)

CHAPTER 8

YOUR GREATEST CALLING: LESSONS FROM THE LIFE OF MARY OF BETHANY

Then Mary took about a pint of pure nard, an expensive perfume; she poured it on Jesus' feet and wiped his feet with her hair. And the house was filled with the fragrance of the perfume.

John 12:3

 ANDY

Some years ago, during an especially busy time, I was speaking at a church's weekend away. I crashed into the weekend, exhausted and feeling overwhelmed by all the things I had to do. The next morning I was preaching about relationship with God as our first priority. I spoke about the first commandment – to love God – and how this is our great call as his children. I went on to say that the danger for many of us is not that we will suddenly rebel against or reject Jesus; it's that in all the pressures of life, we will simply become too busy for him. More often, the risk is not that we will deliberately run away from God; it's that we will accidentally drift away.

As I was talking, it suddenly hit me like a freight train: this was a pretty good description of my current relationship with God! I was so busy doing things *for* him, that I had little time to be *with* him. My weeks were filled with useful-looking activities but I could count on one hand the times I had recently come to Jesus with no agenda. Without meaning to, I had become too busy for Jesus. It is, of course, possible to be busy *and* on fire for God , but that wasn't my situation. Loving God had become 'doing things' for God. I had lost my way.

Years later I still remember the drive home from that retreat centre. I prayed, poured my heart out and repented. I vowed I would never again be too busy to be near my Saviour. I wish I could say that since then I have 'cracked it', but it remains a constant challenge for me to keep the main thing the main thing.

Our Great Calling

For many of us, when we become Christians, our immediate question is about what God wants us to 'do' for him. This is an important question to ask. However it is a little like a couple getting married and thinking the main purpose of their relationship is to do things for the other. That is no doubt an important part of any healthy marriage, but if the couple miss the fact that they have married in order to enjoy and appreciate the other person then pretty soon 'doing things' for the other will be through gritted teeth; an act of will and discipline rather than love and joy.

MIKE

Soon after Andy and Beth were married the three of us went away to speak and lead worship at a camp in the middle of the countryside. We were given a hut to share with two bedrooms. There was no TV or radio and no internet coverage. I was in one room and Andy and Beth were in the other. There was a very thin wall between the two rooms. It is amazing what you can hear through a thin wall late at night when there is no background noise. Especially when you are listening through a glass up against the wall ...

This is what I heard:

Andy: 'Oh Beth, when you sing it is like listening to the voice of an angel.'

Beth: 'Oh Andy, I love listening to you preach. You are so eloquent and deep. And you wear such tight t-shirts ...'

Andy: 'Oh Beth, the way you strum your guitar makes me go weak at the knees. When you change key my heart misses a beat.'

Beth: 'Oh Andy, when you get all passionate in your talks and your lip trembles and you look like you are going to cry, I just want to run up to you and give you a big kiss.'

And so it went on. And on and on and on ... I got bored and went for a walk. What were they doing? They were praising each other, thanking each other, expressing their adoration of each other.

Our first lifeline showed us that John was transformed as he discovered that God delighted in him. Our final lifeline shows we are changed as we delight in God

This is the essence of a relationship of love; the Biblical word for it is worship.

The astonishing truth is this: *We were made to glorify God by enjoying him.*

If we have missed this, then we have missed our greatest calling in life!

Our first lifeline showed us that John was transformed as he discovered that God delighted *in him*. Our final lifeline shows we are changed as we delight *in God*.

The Biblical description of worship is double-sided:

– Worship is a lifestyle. We glorify our God as we live lives that reveal his character and demonstrate his love to our world. Paul writes: 'offer your bodies as a living sacrifice, holy and pleasing to God – this is your true and proper worship' (Rom. 12:1).

– Worship is also particular moments of devotion, when everything else is put on pause and we surrender ourselves to glorifying our God. 'Then those who were in the boat worshipped him, saying, "Truly you are the Son of God"' (Matt. 14:33).

Many of us understand that our lifestyle matters, but we under-value moments of devotion. This chapter is about worship as a particular moment of intimacy with God. As with Andy and Beth, this worship is essentially the expression of our love and devotion. It is recounting to God his attributes: his holiness, majesty, purity, compassion, mercy and grace. It is also thanking him for all his wonderful deeds. It is rejoicing in our relationship with our Father and simply being in his presence. Those who don't know him will find it difficult to understand; however worship is a far more practical, life-changing and necessary part of what it means to follow Jesus than many of us realise.

Our final guide, and our teacher on worship, is Mary of Bethany.

Mary's Story

At Jesus' Feet

Having a chat with Mary would, after a short time, help many of us change the way we relate to God. Everything about her story shows she understood what mattered to Jesus and that she was, in this respect, unique among Jesus' friends.

Mary, Martha and their brother Lazarus were three of Jesus' closest friends. They lived in a village near Jerusalem called Bethany. Whenever Jesus was in the area, he would stay with them. Once Jesus was teaching a group of his disciples in their home. Mary sat at his feet with the disciples, listening; Martha on the other hand, rushed around busily preparing things. She cleaned the dishes, made cups of tea and put dinner in the oven. Finally, resenting all the effort she was making whilst Mary sat around, she asked Jesus to 'have a word' with her sister: 'Tell her to help me!' (Luke 10:40). Martha was probably hoping Jesus would share a parable about a lazy sibling who didn't do any work and came to a nasty end. Instead, Jesus gently but firmly corrected her: '"Martha, Martha," the Lord answered, "you are worried and upset about many things, but few things are needed – or indeed only one. Mary has chosen what is better, and it will not be taken away from her"' (vv. 41-42).

It is good to serve Jesus, it is best to sit with him

Ouch! Do these words describe us? 'Worried and upset about many things.' We know we both relate to them! Consider Jesus' words about Mary, she has 'chosen what is better'. It is good to serve Jesus; it is *best* to sit with him.

The Dinner Party

Time passed, and Jesus performed a miracle when he raised Lazarus from the dead. He then visited Bethany, where Simon the Leper, one of Mary's neighbours, held a party for Jesus.[41] This party was

41   Both Matthew 26:6-13 and John 12:1-11 tell the story of Jesus' being

something special; it was held 'in Jesus' honour' and must have been a treat (John 12:2). Jesus attended lots of dinners. At some, people were trying to trick him into saying something they could use against him (Luke 14:1). At others, Jesus was reaching out to those on the edge of society (Matt. 9:10-11; Luke 19:5). At still others, like the Last Supper or the resurrection breakfast, Jesus himself was the host (John 21:12). This dinner, however, was a party thrown by his friends to celebrate him!

At the dinner we are told: 'Martha served, while Lazarus was among those reclining at the table with him.' In its right place, it is a good thing to serve; in fact, for any gathering where Jesus is celebrated to be possible, people need to serve. Lazarus was, it seems, just relaxing and enjoying the party. Given that he had recently been dead for four days, we can probably make allowances for this. Perhaps someone at this dinner leaned over to Lazarus asking how he was feeling; Laz replied, 'Like death warmed up,' and a phrase was born. Perhaps not. So, it was a pleasant evening for everyone. Then Mary walked in and stunned them all:

'Mary took about a pint of pure nard, an expensive perfume; she poured it on Jesus' feet and wiped his feet with her hair. And the house was filled with the fragrance of the perfume' (John 12:3).

Mary's act was not normal behaviour! People did not wander around meals in the Middle East carrying giant bottles of Chanel and pouring them over each other. We are told that the perfume was worth *a year's wages*. The average annual wage today is around

---

anointed in Bethany shortly before he was arrested. The core details are the same but the stories are told from different perspectives, it's helpful to combine them to get a fuller picture.

£25,000. The family in Bethany were not wealthy – this was probably their life savings; it may well have been a family heirloom. Quite possibly it was Mary's pension plan. She could have been meaning to live from the proceeds of the perfume in her old age. That was, until she strode into the party and poured the lot all over Jesus.

True Worship

It can be easy to read a Biblical story without appreciating the impact it may have had on those who were there at the time. The two of us have always had trouble trying to start the services in our church. Our congregation has something of a discipline problem. They love chatting to each other and drinking coffee, and they do not respect our authority. When we announce we are going to begin, the buzz in the room increases rather than decreases. We think they do this on purpose; they take great pleasure in assuring us that they do.

Suppose at our next service we were to announce to the church, 'Hey everyone, we have £25,000 in cash here!' We imagine that might get their attention. They would rush to sit down, a hush would fall over the room, and for the first time ever the front row would be full. Then imagine we pour petrol over the pile of banknotes. Andy announces: 'The Bible tells us to offer a "sacrifice of praise" to God. As a way of living this out we are going to burn this cash for Jesus!' Before anyone could stop him, Mike lights a match and casually flicks it toward the fuel-doused fortune. BOOM! It goes up in smoke as the band clicks into *Oh Happy Day!*

In a scenario such as this most of us would leap out of our seats shouting 'Noooo!' For some of us, that money could have been a house deposit; for others a way of helping those in need. To all of us, it would seem a huge, expensive *waste*. Were the two of us to actually do this, the money wouldn't be the only thing to go up in flames.

Do we think the people at the party reacted any differently?

Were they any less shocked?

We picture Lazarus reclining at the table, trying to make up his mind whether he would like a stuffed vine leaf or some dates, thinking 'Which did I miss most whilst I was dead?' Suddenly, out of the corner of his eye he sees Mary: 'Oh, there's Mary. What's that she's carrying? It looks like our life savings. That's strange; we normally keep that hidden away. Perhaps she wants to show people.

'Ah, she's heading for Jesus; maybe she wants to give him a drop. She's so generous … wait a minute! *What!?!*' Suddenly Lazarus isn't reclining anymore, he is sitting bolt upright wondering if Jesus can resurrect pints of nard.

Mary's worship shocked the room. What does true worship look like today? Strange as it sounds, it looks like this.

Worship Is Costly

Jesus' Priority

John tells us that Judas objected to Mary's extravagance; he used to steal from the money bag and saw this as potential profit being poured away. Matthew, however, records that *all* the disciples were indignant. Even the disciples who loved Jesus could not believe what Mary had done! "'Why this waste?" they asked. "This perfume could have been sold at a high price and the money given to the poor'" (Matt. 26:8-9).

This word 'waste' implies too much is given for too little.[42] If we were to spend £100 on something that was only worth £1 it would be a waste. In the disciples' eyes, Mary *had just given Jesus too much.* When it comes to worship today we are not so very different from the disciples. We might wonder, 'Why waste all this time singing songs and praising God?' – 'Couldn't we be feeding the poor, sharing the gospel or reading our Bibles?' – 'Wouldn't God want us to be *out there* changing the world?' We ask questions like this because we think God values our service to him more than our celebration of him. We think Jesus is first interested in *practical, useful outcomes.* Jesus' response to Mary's action shows this is not the case.

The moment Mary was criticised, Jesus leapt to her defence, saying "Why are you bothering this woman? She has done a beautiful thing to me. The poor you will always have with you, but you will not always have me. When she poured this perfume on my body, she did it to prepare me for burial. Truly I tell you, wherever this gospel is preached throughout the world, what she has done will also be told, in memory of her" (Matt. 26:10-13).

In his classic book *The Normal Christian Life,* Chinese evangelist Watchman Nee writes about this story: 'Clearly … in approving

---

42   Watchman Nee, *The Normal Christian Life* (Tyndale House, 1977) 269.

Mary's actions at Bethany, the Lord Jesus was laying down one thing as a basis of all service: that you pour out all you have, your very self, *unto him*; and if that should be all he allows you to do, that is enough. It is not first of all a question of whether "the poor" have been helped or not. That will follow, but the first question is: Has the Lord been satisfied?'[43]

So often we misunderstand what Jesus desires – he wants us, our devotion, our affection. He wants to be the one in whom we delight. God wants us to glorify him by enjoying him; he wants us to make that our top priority.

Worship That Satisfies

What might this sort of worship look like today?

Whether we are worshipping by ourselves or with others, for our worship to look like Mary's, it must cost us. What are we bringing to God when we come to worship him? Worship is about pouring ourselves out at Jesus' feet. It is bringing something as precious to us as the perfume was to Mary – our heart, our will, our emotions, our thoughts, our praise – and offering them to God. We may do this through songs; we may do it through tears, or shouts of joy, or sitting in silence. The point is that we stop everything to celebrate God, to enjoy him, to talk to him.

If we get a job at almost any company today, the company attitude will likely be: do your work, perform with efficiency to the best of your ability, and if you have some time left over then you can relate to your colleagues. God's values reverse this. He

---

43   Nee, *The Normal Christian Life*, 274.

says, 'the first commandment is to love me, with all your heart, soul, mind and strength' (see Mark 12:30). To quote Richard Foster: 'The divine priority is worship first, service second.'[44] Of course, often our love for God will be expressed through our service to him, but it means God has the right to tell us to stop everything just to be with him.

When we take this seriously, we may seem to achieve less. People who do not know Jesus will think we are wasting our time.

Our activity for God is always to flow from our adoration of God

Once, when David, Israel's great king and worship leader, had sinned, he was told to offer a sacrifice to God. The location given for the sacrifice was the property of a man named Araunah. Approaching Araunah, David asked to buy the land so he could build an altar upon it. Araunah refused, telling David he would freely give him the land and also the oxen, wood and wheat that would be needed for the sacrifice. 'But King David replied to Araunah, "No, I insist on paying the full price. I will not take for the LORD what is yours, or sacrifice a burnt offering that costs me nothing"' (1 Chron. 21:24). Worship that is only ever convenient, that requires very little in the way of reordering of our priorities, is not the worship of David, or of Mary. Our activity *for* God is always to flow from our adoration *of* God.

---

44   Richard Foster, *Celebration of Discipline* (Hodder & Stoughton, 2008) 200.

Sometimes the cost of worship can be something as simple as choosing to praise God when we do not feel like doing so. In Acts 16:16-40 Paul and his friend Silas had been arrested, severely beaten and thrown into prison. They were in stocks and chains, in the darkest part of the prison. Were we in that situation we would have been trying to call Amnesty International. But we read this of Paul and Silas: 'About midnight Paul and Silas were praying and singing hymns to God' (Acts 16:25). In the middle of the jail, with chains on their wrists, they worshipped God. That's worship that costs! The prisoners around them must have been shocked, 'Why waste your energy?' they must have thought, 'God has clearly abandoned you.'

In order to worship like this there has to be a clear establishing of priorities. It can be tempting to want to cram every moment of every day with activity. We think that this is how we 'get ahead' in the world and, sadly, in the church as well. We will, if we step out of this mindset, find that less appears to be achieved. People around us who don't take this time with God will, on one level, 'move ahead' of us.

We are convinced, however, that we will never regret putting Jesus first in this way. It is what Jesus *wants* from us.

MIKE

Every now and then I meet someone who has the aroma of Jesus. Just being with them causes me to want to pray more, give more and love more. Their extravagant love for Jesus draws me both to them and to Jesus. Hilda Batchelor was one of those people. I was a young youth pastor at St Andrew's Church in Chorleywood and Hilda was a very elderly member of the church. She was a regular sight in the village, walking slowly with her Zimmer frame and seemingly having time to talk to everyone.

I had recently become the youth pastor and felt very important. You might say I was full of self-importance. Then one Sunday the Lord and Hilda ambushed me. It was about forty-five minutes before the morning service and I was busily dashing around doing 'Important Youth Pastor Things'. Out of the corner of my eye I noticed Hilda arrive and park herself and her Zimmer frame on the back row. Hilda often arrived early for the services. I was rushing past her when I heard her say, 'Mike, do you have a minute?' My heart sank. It was rarely just a minute with Hilda. Anyway she wasn't my department. I did youth not the 'Waiting for God' squad.

I didn't want to be rude so I said, 'Hilda, it really will have to be a minute. I am very busy doing important work.' She patted the seat next to her and said, 'Come and sit here, I want to tell you something.' I sat down with a heavy heart. Hilda turned to me and said, 'Mike, isn't Jesus wonderful? I so love our saviour. I love coming to church early and praying for everyone as they walk through the door, that they would know how much our Lord Jesus loves them. If ever you are walking past my house and have time, just pop in.' Then she leaned over conspiratorially and said, 'The back door is always unlocked. We can worship our wonderful saviour together.'

I sat there for a moment and all of a sudden I had the overwhelming desire to become a Christian! I realised what my situation was. I was busy rushing around doing 'important' things for God. Hilda was enjoying him. She loved sitting in his presence. She loved spending time with her king who was also her friend.

There was a smell about Hilda and it had nothing to do with her age. It was the aroma of Christ. The perfume of devoted love

Hilda was not too busy for Jesus. She loved him extravagantly and poured out her love to him regularly. She was ready for heaven. There was a smell about Hilda and it had nothing to do with her age. It was the aroma of Christ. The perfume of devoted love.

It seems so extravagant. So extreme. So wasteful even. However, for those of us who know him, it is the only fitting response. Do we think Mary ever regretted pouring her life savings over her saviour?

Worship Is Intimate

The scene in the room at Bethany was nothing if not intimate – almost awkwardly so for the onlookers! Mary did not just throw perfume over Jesus' feet from a distance and then walk away. She proceeded to get down on her knees, put her face next to his toes and wipe them with her hair. Had any British people been in the room at this point they would have suddenly needed to make an urgent phone call.

If worship is about relationship then it has to be about closeness with God.

Richard Foster says that, 'To worship is to experience Reality, to touch Life. It is to know, to feel, to experience the resurrected Christ in the midst of the gathered community.'[45] In worship we meet with Jesus; we are filled with the Spirit; we are caught up in love for the Father. We *encounter* God. This is not about singing songs *about* God; it is about meeting *with* him.

Much of what we the authors know about worship we learned from the early Vineyard movement. We recently watched an interview with some of the founders of the movement, Carol Wimber and Bob and Penny Fulton. They spoke of how in the early days they began to gather in someone's home and sing simple love songs to Jesus. As they did so the presence of God filled the room. They described the amazing intimacy with God that they would experience in those moments. They began to close their eyes as they worshipped – this was long before closing your eyes in worship was the done thing. They did so because it was such a poignant and personal encounter with the Lord that it felt like an intrusion to watch another worship. We wonder how many people in the room at Bethany had to look away as Mary so unashamedly displayed her love for Jesus.

---

45   Foster, *Celebration of Discipline*, 197.

Worship Involves Our Body

If worship is to involve our whole hearts, then it will inevitably involve our bodies. Perhaps it is an obvious point to make, but Mary's act was a very physical one: the posture of her body, the caress of her hair and the smell of the perfume. We can make the mistake of thinking of worship as such a 'spiritual' thing that we remove our bodies from the picture. The Bible does not separate the physical from the spiritual; this is especially clear when it comes to worship. We are told to love God with all our heart, soul, mind and *strength* (Deut. 6:5). David, when he worshipped the Lord before the crowd, danced 'with all his might' (2 Sam. 6:14).

The Biblical language for worship uses very physical terms: 'The root meaning for the Hebrew word we translate as *worship* is "to prostrate." The word *bless* literally means "to kneel." *Thanksgiving* refers to "an extension of the hand."'[46] The psalms command us to sing, and throughout the Bible people are lying, standing, kneeling, lifting their hands, dancing, bowing and playing any instrument they can get their hands on.

—————————— ANDY ——————————

I remember the first time I went to a Christian meeting where someone lifted their hands. 'What a weirdo,' I thought; 'Even if I

---

46   Foster, *Celebration of Discipline*, 208.

become a Christian I'm *never* going to do that!' Expressive worship does seem strange until we remember it is natural for us to express what we want with our bodies. My son, Judah, has just learned to walk. He toddles around from room to room in our home. Yesterday I was in the kitchen when he ambled in and struck a 'worship pose'. Walking right up to me, he looked up, lifted his arms, and held both hands high above his head. It was a pose that said, 'Pick me up, Dad, I want to be close.'

Worship is a physical thing, as much as it's something of the spirit. This is not to say that it has to involve certain prescribed actions – we have noticed in our worship services that at any one time people can be crying, kneeling or dancing – it is to say it should be whole-hearted, which is likely to involve the whole body![47]

Worship Takes Time

One thing we might miss as we read Mary's story is how long her interaction with Jesus must have taken. This was a lot of perfume. Hair doesn't just absorb large quantities of oil. It's a fair inference that this wasn't over in thirty seconds. Too often in our fast paced world we miss the importance of taking real, unrestricted time with Jesus.

---

47   Foster, *Celebration of Discipline*, 209.

---------------------------- ANDY ----------------------------

Once, when Beth and I were in Rome, we visited the Vatican
Museum. We decided to go mainly so that we could see the famous
Sistine Chapel. Neither of us are especially into art; we just wanted
to be able to *say* we'd seen the Sistine Chapel. The museum is
designed like a maze, with the chapel right at the end. For a couple
of hours we raced down corridors lined with sculptures and rushed
passed the countless masterpieces that hung on the walls. Finally
we got to the chapel. We spent about ten minutes craning our
necks and looking up at Michelangelo's handiwork, then we headed
off to find that other Italian masterpiece: pizza. We saw an awful
lot at the Vatican, but we didn't *adore* a single thing. Why?
Adoration takes time; time we weren't willing to give.

When my son Judah reaches for a cuddle, I don't just pick him
up for a few seconds and then put him down. To experience
closeness with someone else, we need to be willing to linger; to stop
watching the clock; to be more concerned with our closeness to
them than the jobs we have to do next. True worship, alone and
corporately, is never to be rushed.

True Worship Changes The Atmosphere

We Are Changed

As a result of Mary's act, we are told, the whole house was filled
with the fragrance of the perfume. When relationship with Jesus is

at the centre of our lives, when our main ambition is to express our love for him, this releases a perfume that fills us, and affects those around us.

We began by saying worship is not about 'practical outcomes' and it isn't; it's about glorifying the one we love. But when we obey the first commandment, 'love the Lord your God with all your heart, soul, mind and strength', everything flows from it. We have already made the point that we experience true change not by gritting our teeth but by falling in love. Since marrying Beth, Andy has spent more hours in IKEA than he ever thought he would. Beth is a frustrated interior designer, and because he loves her, Andy has over the years become a lover of Swedish furniture.

This is how holiness happens. It is not about gritting our teeth and summoning all our energy to keep to our latest resolution. As our love for Jesus grows we begin to love the things that he loves: mercy, kindness, gentleness, generosity. And we grow to hate the things that he hates: injustice, cruelty, using another human being to gratify our selfish desires. To love God is to change.

The Heart of Worship

Jesus told a room full of indignant disciples that wherever the gospel is preached, Mary's story would be told. This is because the purpose of the gospel is that, like Mary, people might extravagantly pour their lives out to Jesus.

We have a choice as to how we live. We can grit our teeth, fill our diaries, and attempt to achieve things for Jesus. Or we can understand, on a deep level, that God seeks worshippers, and that, in truth, it is worshippers who change the world.

———————————————— MIKE ————————————————

We planted our church, Soul Survivor Watford, in 1993. Matt Redman was our first worship pastor. From the beginning the worship of God was very important to us and one of our core values. For the first few years we had some wonderful times of worship. It was our experience that the Lord did 'inhabit the praises of his people'. We were passionate, engaged and expressive as we sang our songs of devotion. Then after a few years I noticed something begin to change. We were not as fervent in our praise; not as expressive in our adoration. Folk stopped engaging and seemed at times to be going through the motions.

As the pastor I became increasingly concerned about this and attempted to analyse what was wrong. My first conclusion was that the volume was too loud. I went to the guy who ran our PA and told him to turn it down. He initially refused. I sat on him. He agreed. It made no difference. I continued my analysis. My next conclusion was that we were singing the songs too slowly. The music was dragging. I spoke to Matt and told him to speed it up. He told me to speak to the drummer. I instructed the drummer to watch my foot and to keep up with my stamping in the front row.

The only discernible difference was that we finished the meeting ten minutes early.

Finally, I began to listen to the conversations we were having about our sung worship, and it was disturbing. We were saying things like, 'The worship didn't do anything for me today'; 'I don't like that song'; 'I prefer the other bass player.' I realised to my horror that we had become consumers of worship rather than givers of worship. Somehow we had turned it into something that was more for us than for him, an activity that we thought should bless us rather than our king. I knew enough to realise this was serious.

I began a teaching series on worship, reminding us that we were required to bring a sacrifice of praise, and asked us to consider whether we were coming with an attitude to give to God or relying on Matt and the band to do the work for us. For some reason we did not see a lot of change. I became desperate. I was so desperate that I did a crazy thing. I told the church that for a while Matt and the band would not lead us. If no one came with an offering of praise or thanksgiving or confession or adoration, than we would all sit in silence.

The first meeting was agony. There was almost total silence. At the end, one of my friends informed me that if we had many more meetings like that then we would not have a church left as everyone would leave and go somewhere else. My honest response was that I would rather close the church than lead a congregation that does not worship Jesus. After a while, however, we began to understand. People started bringing prayers, readings and songs.

The atmosphere was electric again. We had moved back from an empty ritual to engagement. We sensed his nearness. We once again poured out our hearts. We were once again extravagant in our praise.

I asked Matt to begin to lead us again. The first Sunday he led acoustically, on his own. He began singing a song he had written in the middle of our agony. The first verse and chorus go like this:

> When the music fades, all is stripped away,
> And I simply come,
> Longing just to bring something that's of worth,
> That will bless your heart.
> I'll bring you more than a song
> For a song in itself is not what you have required.
> You search much deeper within,
> Through the way things appear,
> You're looking into my heart.
>
> I'm coming back to the heart of worship
> and it's all about you, it's all about you Jesus.
> I'm sorry Lord for the thing I've made it
> when it's all about you, it's all about you Jesus.[48]

This song expressed it perfectly. I have to confess, however, I told Matt that he would only be able to sing this song at our

---

48   Matt Redman, 'The Heart of Worship' © 1997, Thankyou Music.

church because no one else would understand it. How wrong I was!

If Mary of Bethany were sitting with us today, what would she want to say? Maybe it would go something like this: 'It is good to serve Jesus by serving people. He loves it when we feed the hungry, tell people the good news and help others. However, we will love people more when we love Jesus more. Love your family, friends, community and the world you are a part of. But love Jesus first. As you do, your love for everything he cares about will grow until it overflows. And don't just love him. Love him extravagantly. Why? Because he loved you extravagantly. He poured out his life for us on the cross, and in response we pour the perfume of our praise over him.'

The One They Worshipped

The risk in looking at Mary's action is that we see Mary more than the one to whom she was offering her worship: the unique Jesus Christ. Whether they knew him in person or not, Jesus' story is woven throughout the characters we have met in this book.

It was Jesus' love that transformed John from the angry, insecure, violent man he was, into the Apostle of Love. The kindness of Jesus is evident in the way God met Elijah, seeking relationship with him in the quiet place. Ruth's vow to Naomi points to the life Jesus lived as the one who goes with us, stays with us and dies for us. Like Joseph, Jesus was faithful throughout his trials. He was betrayed, in his case, to the prison of death, only to be resurrected to the seat of ultimate power. That which we meant to harm him, the Father meant for our good. Jesus is the Good Shepherd, fulfilling that which his great ancestor David foretold and, in an imperfect way, lived out. Facing greater tests than Daniel ever could, Jesus stood firm in a world that attempted to seduce and intimidate him. And in contrast to Samson, he was the perfect Nazirite, flawlessly fulfilling his YES to his Father, and doing so on our behalf that we might never be separated from the love of God.

> *Life with God is to be lived out in the gritty, raw, messy, unglamorous, unpredictable, difficult, glorious every day*

Life with God is to be lived out in the gritty, raw, messy, unglamorous, unpredictable, difficult, glorious every day. To this end, the guides we have spent time with aid us. They, and many more in the Bible, have been there before us. The practical trials we face today may take new forms on the surface, but scratch beneath and they are age-old challenges. We will at times be daunted. But never forget, the God of John, Elijah, Ruth, Joseph, David, Daniel, Samson and Mary is *your God*. He is with you now. It is he who loves you, will be faithful to you, and will keep you under the shadow of his wing. You need not be afraid; he will never leave you, he will never forsake you. With your trust placed in him who is beside, behind and before you, you can be at peace: your life too, will point to him.

Read Mary's Lifeline for Yourself

Mary's appearances in the gospels are:

- Mary sitting at the feet of Jesus, Luke 10:38-42.
- Mary's involvement with the death and resurrection of Lazarus, John 11:1-44.
- The anointing of Jesus, John 12:2-8; see also Matthew 26:6-13.

Group questions

1. 'The divine priority is worship first, service second.' Do you agree? Why?
2. In what ways have you found your 'Christian activity' has hindered your friendship with God? What practical steps can you take to change this?
3. Have you ever met someone, like our friend Hilda, who makes you want to get to know both them and Jesus better? Describe them.
4. Can you articulate what your equivalent to pouring expensive perfume over Jesus would be?
5. Have you or your church had a time when you have realised that you needed to come back to the heart of worship, which is Jesus? Can you describe that time?
6. Which of the characters or stories in *Lifelines* can you relate to the most? Why?